The 500 Hidden Secrets of

BOSTON

INTRODUCTION

This book acts as a guide, inviting readers to discover the city of Boston beyond its famous landmarks. While Boston is celebrated for its rich history, prestigious universities, and passionate sports culture, this guide delves into the often-overlooked attractions that define the city's true character.

Journeying through charming neighborhoods like Brookline, Harvard Square, Beacon Hill, and Charlestown, it highlights inviting coffee shops, boutique bookstores, and intimate art galleries, enriched with historical anecdotes. It explores Boston's culinary diversity, featuring upscale brunch spots, iconic eateries run by renowned chefs that truly live up to their reputation, and family-owned restaurants across the city, including those in the historic North End Italian district. For those looking to enjoy Boston's outdoors, the guide reveals hidden urban parks, scenic walking trails, and ideal picnic spots with beautiful skyline views of Boston and Cambridge. For the culturally curious, it showcases local festivals, underground music venues, and theaters presenting diverse performances. Moreover, it sheds light on Boston's innovative side by featuring makerspaces, tech hubs, and distinctive university buildings that reflect the city's role as a leader in education and innovation.

By weaving together these elements, the book aims to capture a city constantly evolving yet deeply rooted in tradition. While it won't capture everything there is to do or enjoy in Boston, it draws from personal experiences and provides detailed recommendations, encouraging both visitors and longtime residents to explore beyond the typical tourist spots.

THE AUTHOR

Born in Ukraine, Natalia Ivanytsky immigrated to the U.S. with her family at age six. Her parents nurtured a love for travel through summer road trips across the country. Her passion for exploration was further ignited during a study abroad semester in Spain and an international work assignment in Australia. Since then, she has journeyed to numerous countries across the world. While her itineraries have evolved, she's relied on Excel for her meticulous planning, and photography has become a way to cherish her memories.

Amidst her travels, Natalia realized she hadn't fully explored her own backyard, a realization magnified during COVID-19. Boston has been her home since attending Boston College, living in neighborhoods like Brookline, Back Bay, South End, and Charlestown. Natalia has wandered Boston's streets, seeking out the cutest coffee shops, indulging in brunch spots with close friends, and discovering new green spaces to walk her dog. In writing this book, she aims to showcase Boston's vibrant culture beyond its renowned sports and history, and is continually seeking new, unexplored places.

The author would like to send a special thanks to her parents, Olha and Yuri, for instilling a love of travel; to her husband, Ryan, always up for any adventure; and to her closest Boston friends for always being open to try new places to eat and drink. She would also like to thank the team at Luster, especially Dettie Luyten, for her guidance and support in writing this book, and Claudia Uripos, for capturing the beauty of Boston through her photographs.

HOW TO USE THIS BOOK

This guide lists 500 things you need to know about Boston in 100 different categories. Most of these are places to visit, with practical information to help you find your way. Others are bits of information that help you get to know the city and its habitants. The aim of this guide is to inspire, not to cover the city from A to Z.

The places listed in the guide are given an address, including the neighborhood (for example Beacon Hill or Harvard Square), and a number. The neighborhood and number allow you to find the locations on the maps at the beginning of the book: first look for the map of the corresponding neighborhood, then look for the right number. A word of caution however: these maps are not detailed enough to allow you to find specific locations in the city. You can obtain an excellent map from any tourist office or in most hotels. Or the addresses can be located on a smartphone.

Please also bear in mind that cities change all the time. The chef who hits a high note one day may be uninspiring on the day you happen to visit. The hotel ecstatically reviewed in this book might suddenly go downhill under a new manager. The bar considered one of the best cocktail bars might be empty on the night you visit. This is obviously a highly personal selection. You might not always agree with it. If you want to leave a comment, recommend a bar or reveal your favorite secret place, please visit the website *the500hiddensecrets.com* – you'll also find free tips and the latest news about the series there – or follow @500hiddensecrets on Instagram or Facebook and leave a comment.

DOWNLOAD TWO FREE WALKS

As well as hand-picking 500 hidden secrets in Boston, author Natalia Ivanytsky has also mapped out two city walks. These walks are a great way to explore the city, and will lead you past several of the addresses in the book. Each walk is led by a specific theme that defines Boston in some way: its maritime history and its literary legacy. The walks are available as digital downloads in the *the500hiddensecrets.com* bookshop. As the owner of this book, you get them for free by scanning the QR code below:

BOSTON

overview

Map 1

BACK BAY & SOUTH END

EAT – DRINK – SHOP – BUILDINGS – DISCOVER – CULTURE – CHILDREN – SLEEP – WEEKEND – RANDOM

Map 2

WEST END, BEACON HILL, DOWNTOWN & CHINATOWN

EAT – DRINK – SHOP – BUILDINGS – DISCOVER – CULTURE – CHILDREN – SLEEP – WEEKEND – RANDOM

Map 3

NORTH END & WATERFRONT

EAT – DRINK – SHOP – BUILDINGS – DISCOVER – CULTURE – CHILDREN – SLEEP – WEEKEND – RANDOM

Map 4

CHARLESTOWN

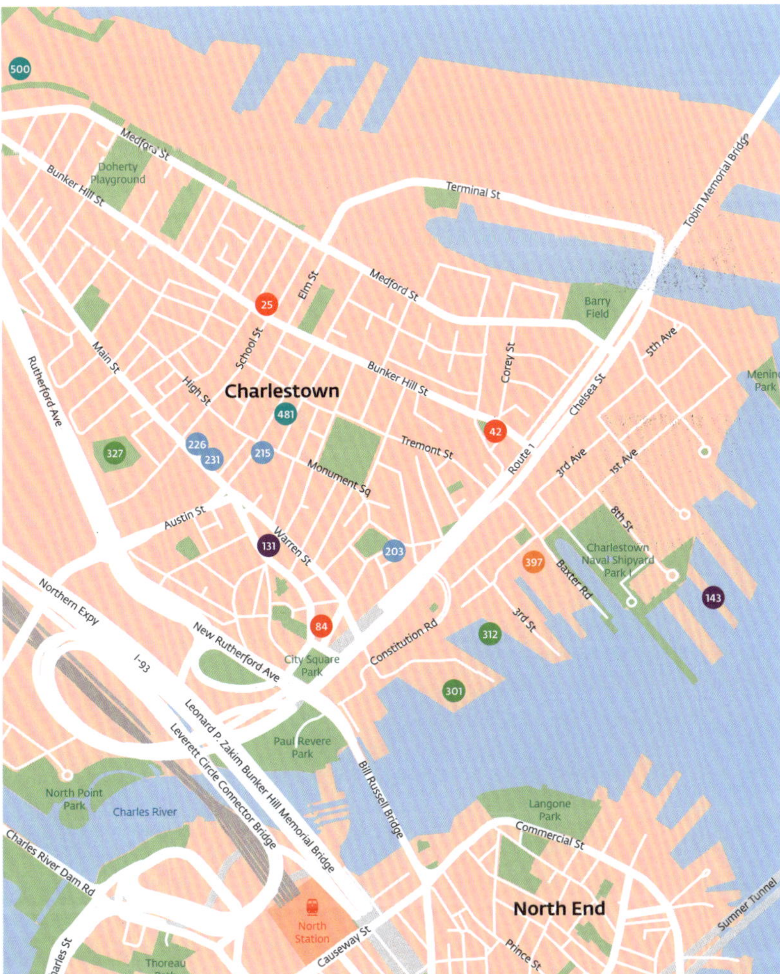

EAT – DRINK – SHOP – BUILDINGS – DISCOVER – CULTURE – CHILDREN – SLEEP – WEEKEND – RANDOM

Map 5

SEAPORT & SOUTH BOSTON

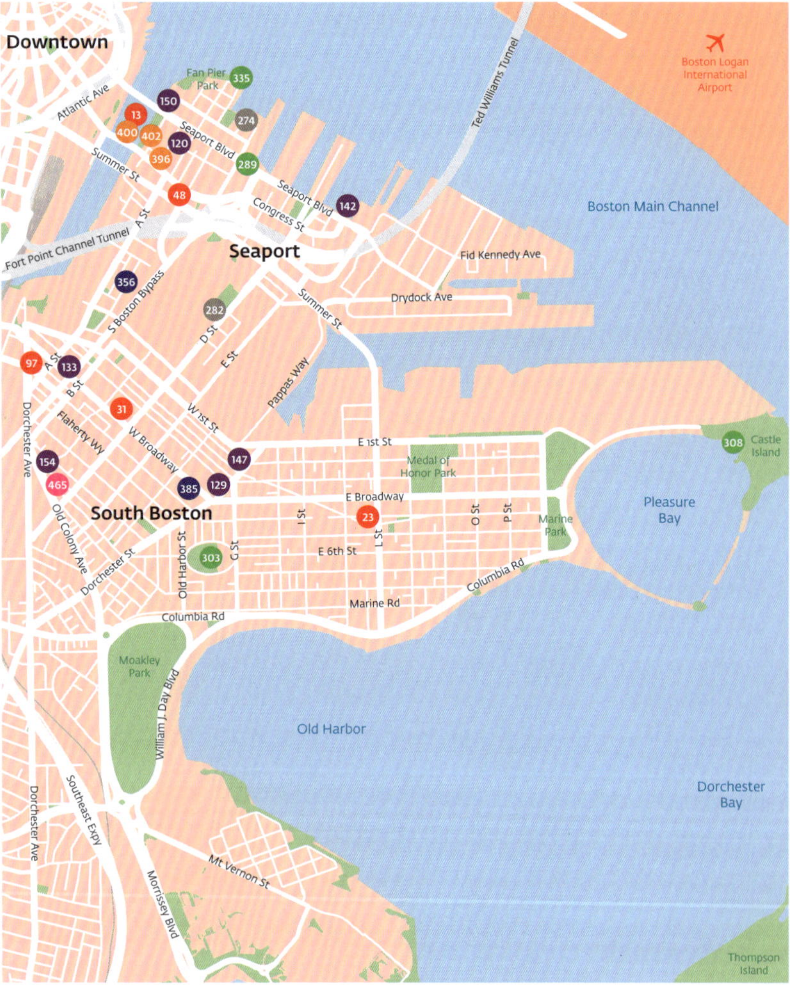

EAT – DRINK – SHOP – BUILDINGS – DISCOVER – CULTURE – CHILDREN – SLEEP – WEEKEND – RANDOM

Map 6

EAST BOSTON

Map 7

BRIGHTON, COOLIDGE CORNER, FENWAY, NEWTON, BROOKLINE, MISSION HILL, JAMAICA PLAIN & WEST ROXBURY

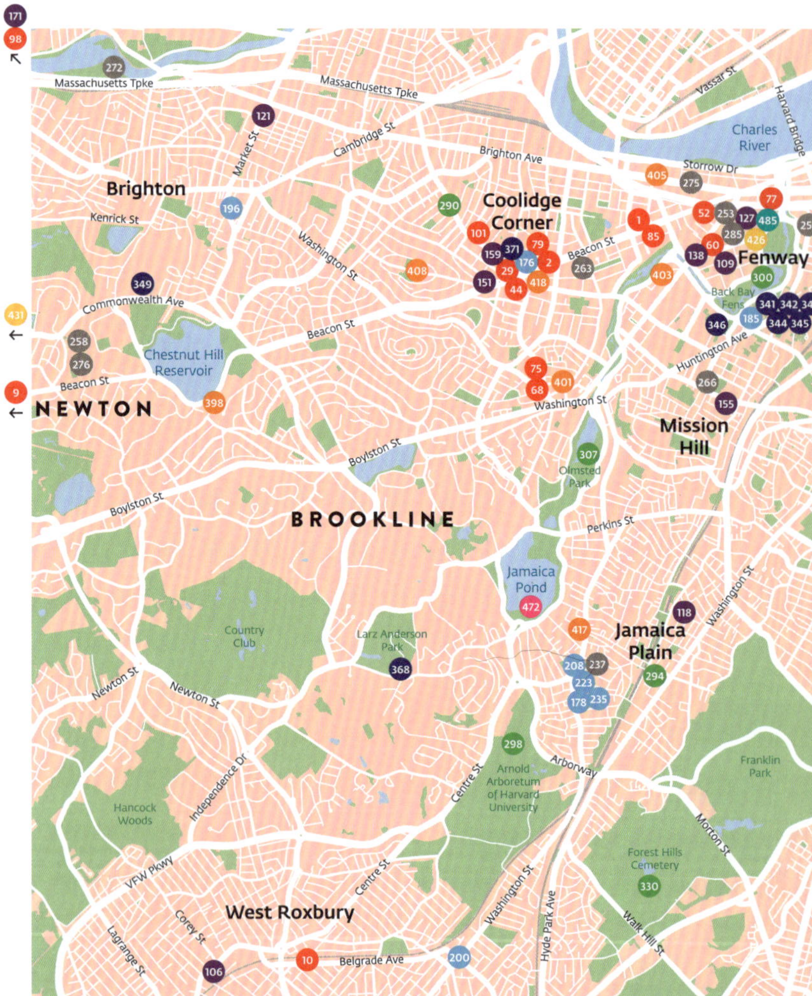

EAT – DRINK – SHOP – BUILDINGS – DISCOVER – CULTURE – CHILDREN – SLEEP – WEEKEND – RANDOM

Map 8

ROXBURY & DORCHESTER

EAT – DRINK – SHOP – BUILDINGS – DISCOVER – CULTURE – CHILDREN – SLEEP – WEEKEND – RANDOM

Map 9

CAMBRIDGE & ALLSTON

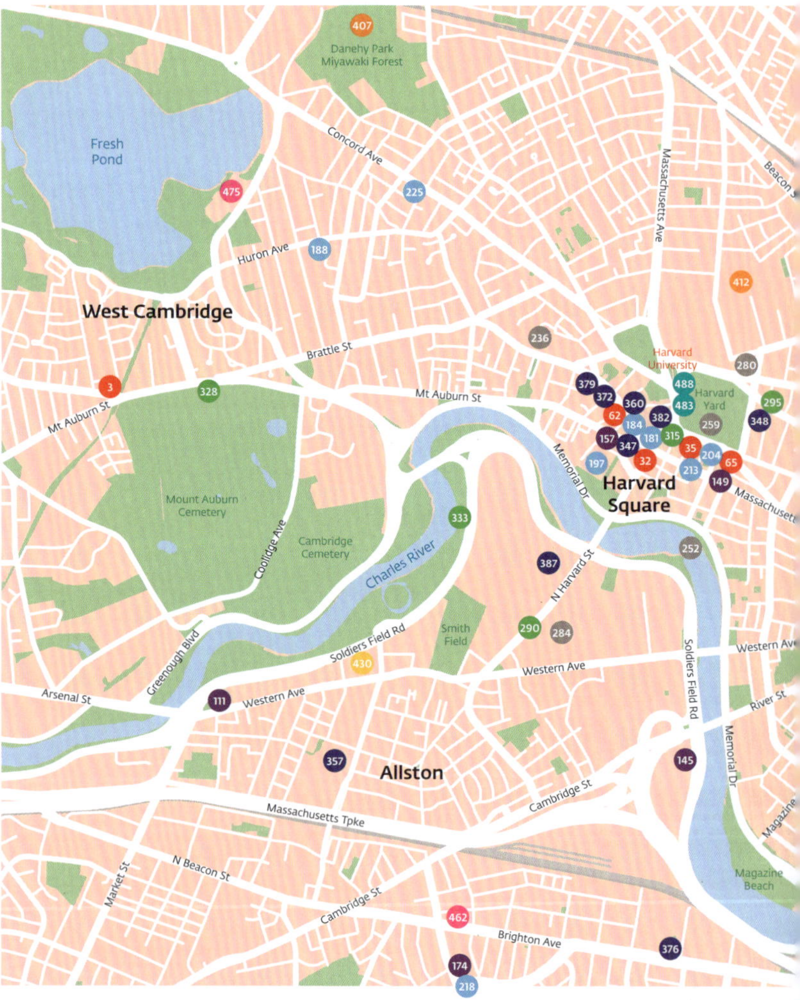

EAT – DRINK – SHOP – BUILDINGS – DISCOVER – CULTURE – CHILDREN – SLEEP – WEEKEND – RANDOM

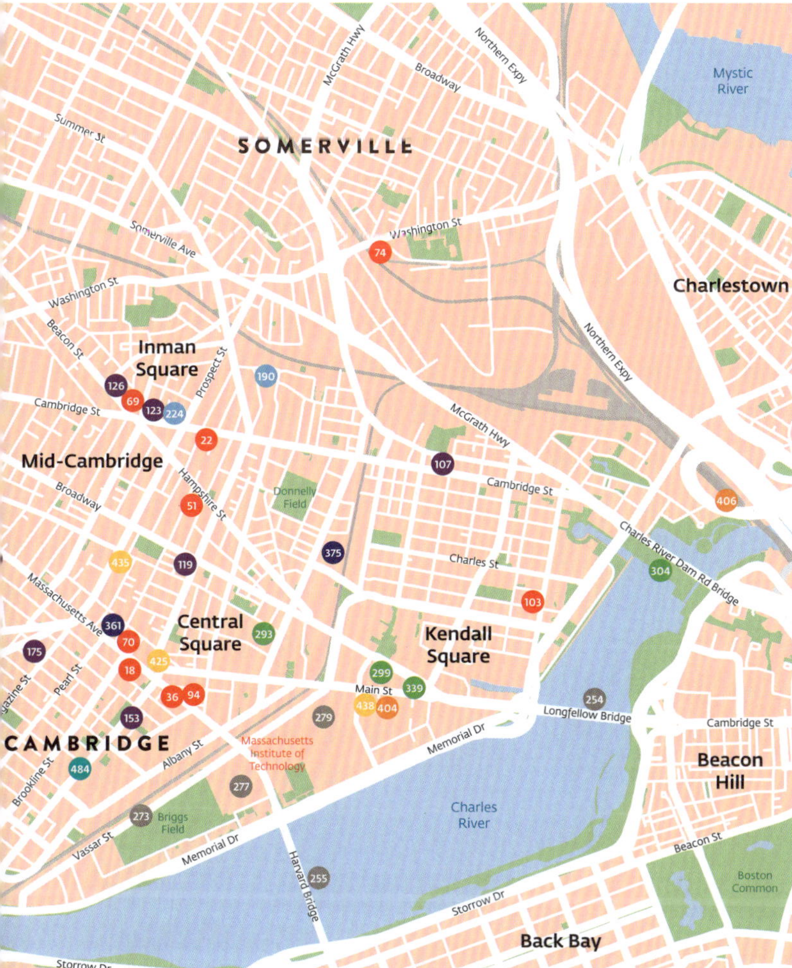

EAT — DRINK — SHOP — BUILDINGS — DISCOVER — CULTURE — CHILDREN — SLEEP — WEEKEND — RANDOM

Map 10

SOMERVILLE

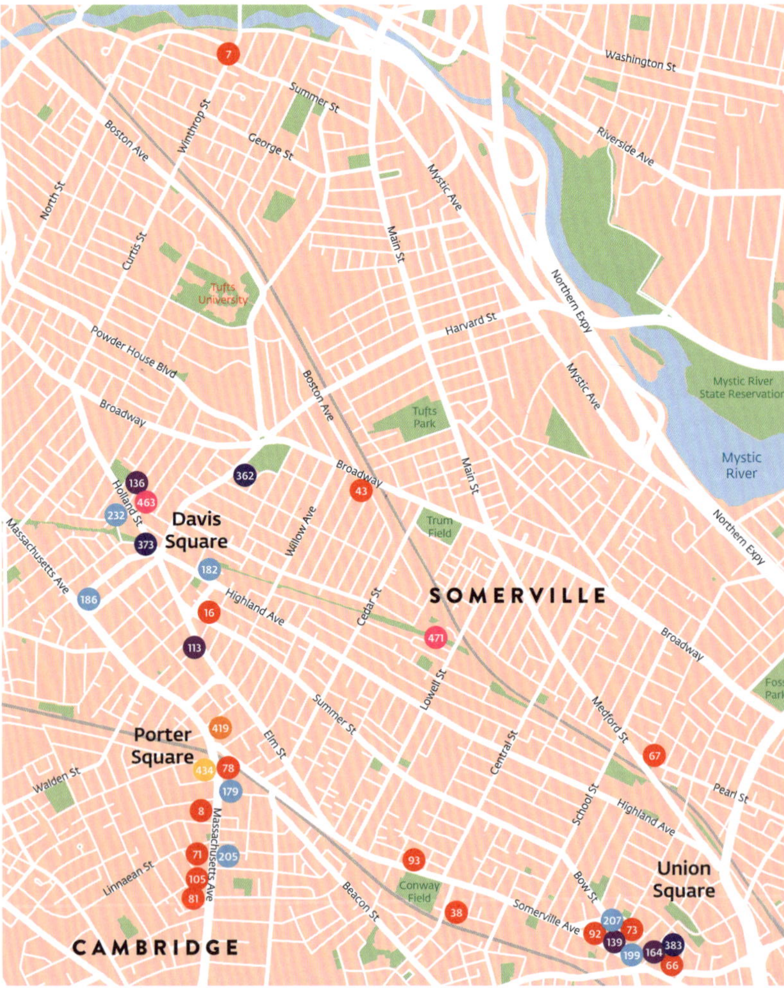

EAT – DRINK – SHOP – BUILDINGS – DISCOVER – CULTURE – CHILDREN – SLEEP – WEEKEND – RANDOM

Map 11
AROUND BOSTON

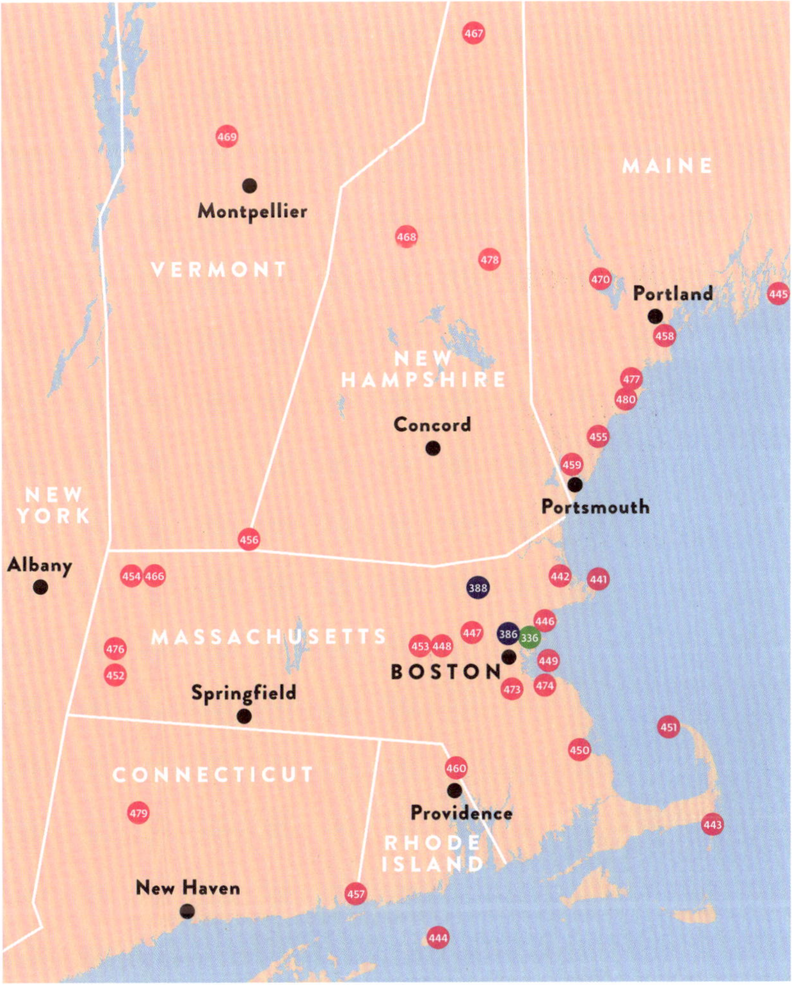

EAT – DRINK – SHOP – BUILDINGS – DISCOVER – CULTURE – CHILDREN – SLEEP – WEEKEND – RANDOM

MONICA'S MERCATO & SALUMERIA

& SALUMERIA
BOSTON
BRUINS

105 PLACES TO EAT OR BUY GOOD FOOD

5 BAKED DELIGHTS
from around the globe

1 **CURRY DONUTS**
AT: JAPONAISE
1020 Beacon St
Brookline ⑦
+1 617 566 7730
japonaise.
squarespace.com

Known as the first Japanese bakery in Boston, Japonaise serves a selection of traditional Japanese delights. However, the standout savory option is the *Kare Pan*, a Japanese curry donut. The curry is delicately spiced, and complemented with a subtly sweet dough, served fresh and warm out of the air fryer.

2 **PASTEIS DE NATA**
AT: FLAKE BAKERY
1298 Beacon St
Coolidge Corner ⑦
+1 617 290 3906
flakebakery.com

Flake specializes in and serves only one treat: Portuguese Pastéis de Nata. These velvety custard tarts, made from egg yolks, sugar and flaky pastry, are baked fresh throughout the day and always served fresh. Their delicate sweetness and crisp crust make stopping at one nearly impossible, so make sure to order at least half a dozen.

3 **MORNING BUN**
AT: SOFRA
1 Belmont St
West Cambridge ⑨
+1 617 661 3161
sofrabakery.com

Sofra is best known for exceptional Middle Eastern flavors, serving a selection of baked goods and takeaway dishes. A local favorite is the morning bun, made of croissant dough filled with cardamom and topped with orange blossom glaze. The citrus notes provide a morning buzz, paired best with a homemade chai or a Turkish coffee.

4 **PAN DULCE**
AT: LOLLY'S BAKERY
158 Bennington St
East Boston ⑥
+1 617 567 9461
@lollysbakery

Lolly's is an authentic Latin American bakery in East Boston, cherished by locals for its delicious pastries. Specializing in *pan dulce*, a staple sweet bread in Latin cuisine, Lolly's offers the city's best *conchas* and exotic guava-filled *pan dulce*, perfect for any occasion. Each pastry on offer is fresh, tasty and affordable.

5 **COCONUT CUSTARD BUN**
AT: HO YUEN BAKERY
54 Beach St
Chinatown ②
+1 617 426 8320

Ho Yuen Bakery is an unassuming bakery on one of Chinatown's busiest streets, but it holds many traditional Chinese delicacies, like the Red Bean Mooncake. But if you're not into red bean paste, try the Coconut Custard Bun, a delightful mix of flaky pastry, chewy custard, and the right hint of sweetness.

5 BOSTON BAGELS
that rival New York

6 **BRICK STREET BAGELS**
312 Shawmut Avenue
South End ①
@brick.street.bagles

After thriving as a pop-up, Brick Street Bagels opened a permanent spot in South End due to overwhelming demand, selling out every weekend. Freshly made each morning, their bagels come in all the favorite flavors. Even though expanded, the bagels still sell out, so make sure to pre-order from their Instagram page.

7 **GOLDILOX BAGELS**
186 Winthrop St
Medford ⑩
+1 617 333 8233
goldiloxbagels.com

The Goldilox bagel strikes the perfect balance between tender and crispy. The shop is open only on weekends, and its popular bagels frequently sell out fast. Look out for the weekend special, like cranberry orange or blueberry lemon, and don't miss their unique pizza bagels.

8 **BAGELSAURUS**
1796 Massachusetts Avenue
Porter Square ⑩
+1 857 285 6103
bagelsaurus.com

Bagelsaurus stands out with bagels crafted from a decades-old sourdough starter, each one handmade and fermented for over 24 hours. The shop offers standard varieties of bagels daily, with specials that rotate weekly. Inventive cream cheeses and spreads, like honey rosemary and basil hummus, complement the bagels.

9 **ROSENFELD'S BAGELS**

1280 Centre St
Newton ⑦
+1 617 527 8080
rosenfeldsbagels.com

Since 1973, Rosenfeld's Bagels in Boston has operated as a traditional kosher bakery, specializing in boiled bagels and hand-mixed spreads. It was founded by a Suffolk Law student with experience in one of New Jersey's top bagel shops. These bagels offer a nostalgic taste of the city for those missing traditional New York bagels.

10 **EXODUS BAGELS**

2 McCraw St
Roslindale ⑦
+1 617 323 3354
exodusbagels.com

For inventive bagel sandwiches, Exodus Bagels is a must. The shop operates through a small pick-up window, where customers can enjoy their bagels on small bucket chairs. Their soft, chewy bagels come with a variety of toppings, including the crowd-favorite Monumental, which features egg, greens, caramelized onion jam, and a choice of avocado or bacon.

8 BAGELSAURUS

14 BEACON HILL BOOKSTORE

5 pinkies up
HIGH TEA *haunts*

11 **ROWES WHARF SEA GRILLE**
70 Rowes Wharf
Waterfront ③
+1 617 856 7744
roweswharf seagrille.com

Overlooking Boston Harbor, this tearoom at Rowes Wharf offers both indoor seating and an outdoor terrace. Housed within the Boston Harbor Hotel, the sophisticated setting pairs perfectly with the refined menu featuring a selection of fine teas, finger sandwiches, and pastries, and a gluten-free option available upon request.

12 **SILVER DOVE AFTERNOON TEA**
24 Tremont St
Downtown ②
+1 781 203 1223
silverdovetea.com

Silver Dove, located inside the historic Langham Hotel, formerly The Federal Reserve Bank of Boston, offers a fully gluten and oat-free, seasonal high tea menu. This elegant setting is perfect for special occasions, providing the perfect excuse to get dressed up to enjoy a refined afternoon with your closest friends.

13 **ABIGAIL'S TEA ROOM**

306 Congress St
Seaport ⑤
+1 866 955 0667
bostonteapartyship.com/tea-room

At the Boston Tea Party Ships & Museum, this waterfront tearoom offers a unique take on traditional high tea. Guests can sample five teas, all representing those destroyed in the 1773 Boston Tea Party. Colonial costumed servers enhance the experience, making it an engaging and educational outing for all ages.

14 **BEACON HILL BOOKSTORE**

71 Charles St
Beacon Hill ②
+1 617 945 4713
bhbooks.com

This bookstore cafe, straight out of a picture book, offers a high tea with lighter food pairings, ideal for a late breakfast or early lunch. It's the perfect end to exploring the rest of the charming bookstore, with its many nooks and crannies, inspired by the rich history of the townhouses scattered throughout Beacon Hill.

15 **COURTYARD TEA ROOM**

AT: BOSTON PUBLIC LIBRARY
700 Boylston St
Back Bay ①
+1 781 763 1360
thecateredaffair.com/courtyard-tea-room

Enjoying high tea in the Boston Public Library's Courtyard Tea Room offers a peaceful way to take in its stunning architecture of the McKim building. The inviting tearoom has a calm setting to sip tea and unwind, while enjoying one of Boston's most iconic spaces. After tea, you can walk through or relax in the outdoor open-air courtyard surrounded by architecture and lush greenery.

5 RETRO VIBE DINERS

16 **ROSEBUD BAR & KITCHEN**
381 Summer St
Davis Square ⑩
+1 617 629 9500
rosebudkitchen.com

Under new ownership, this Davis Square institution seamlessly blends traditional brunch with Indian-inspired flavored dishes. There are unique dishes like Kerala Fried Chicken with Green Chili Waffles and Butter Chicken Pot Pie. For a truly retro dining experience, ask for a seat in the vintage tram car at the front.

16 ROSEBUD BAR & KITCHEN

17 **THEO'S COZY CORNER RESTAURANT**

162 Salem St
North End ③
+1 617 241 0202
@theo1994

Theo's, a Brazilian-owned diner, combines classic American breakfasts with authentic Brazilian treats like *picanha* steak. This no-frills, cash-only spot doesn't take reservations, operating on a one-in, one-out basis. With a cozy capacity of thirty people, the intimate setting matches its inviting name.

18 **VEGGIE GALAXY**

450 Massachusetts Avenue
Central Square ⑨
+1 617 497 1513
veggiegalaxy.com

This retro diner, with a futuristic Jetsons-like exterior, serves up vegetarian and vegan twists on breakfast classics like burritos, biscuits and gravy, and stuffed French toast. The best part? You don't need to be vegetarian or vegan to enjoy their classic diner comfort food.

19 **SOUTH STREET DINER**

178 Kneeland St
Chinatown ②
+1 617 350 0028
southstreetdiner.com

Established in 1947 as the Blue Diner, South Street Diner is a cherished Boston landmark offering 24/7 service. In a city where most establishments close by 2 am, this iconic eatery originally served factory workers but now caters to a lively mix of late-night customers.

20 **MIKE'S CITY DINER**

1714 Washington St
South End ①
+1 617 267 9393
mikescitydiner.com

Mike's, beloved for its classic American comfort food, was purchased in 1995 by Jay Hajj, a Lebanese immigrant and frequent Food Network guest. Jay transformed this once-struggling eatery into a coveted spot, famous for its flavorful corned beef hash. The diner offers a 50s-style decor and generous portions, attracting both locals and visitors.

5 CLASSY BRUNCH *destinations*

21 **KRASI**
48 Gloucester St
Back Bay ①
+1 617 536 0230
krasiboston.com

Krasi's sleek interior and charming Back Bay patio create an inviting brunch spot for lingering with friends. The menu features a twist on traditional Greek meze, with brunch-inspired small plates that are perfect for sharing, and pairs well with their extensive Greek wine list or creative brunch cocktails.

22 **PURITAN & COMPANY**
1164-1166 Cambridge St
Inman Square ⑨
+1 617 615 6195
puritancambridge.com

Brunch at Puritan & Company is ideal for a champagne-worthy afternoon. Feast on a seasonal farm-to-table menu inspired by New England flavors in a cozy, upscale setting with warm wood tones. Standout dishes include the pastry bucket from Cafe Beatrice's pastry chef and the smoked brisket hash, both perfectly paired with a refreshing mimosa pitcher.

23 PETULA'S

81 L St
South Boston ⑤
+1 617 752 4531
petulasboston.com

Petula's is an airy, plant-filled space evoking a European eatery, perfect for brunch on a sunny day. The menu features fresh, locally sourced dishes with a healthy twist, like sweet potato pancakes and an egg sandwich with charred tomato aioli. Complementing the space are marble tables, antique accents, and a showstopping purple bar.

24 SONSIE

327 Newbury St
Back Bay ①
+1 617 351 2500
sonsieboston.com

With French doors and open-air seating overlooking Newbury Street, Sonsie offers a French cafe vibe, perfect for brunch and people watching. It's easy to spend hours enjoying the lively street scene while indulging in sweet breads, like muffins, scones, croissants, and classic breakfast dishes, including French-inspired specialties.

25 WAVERLY

231 Bunker Hill St
Charlestown ④
+1 617 380 6500
waverlycharlestown.com

Tucked away in a residential part of Charlestown, Waverly infuses classic charm into Boston's brunch scene with its cozy wood accents and inviting fireplace. Start your meal with a tempting appetizer like sweet potato croquettes or warm banana bread slathered in maple butter, setting the stage for the savory brunch dishes that follow.

25 **WAVERLY**

5 on-the-go tasty
SANDWICHES

26 **PASTRAMI / CORNED BEEF SANDWICH**
AT: SAM LAGRASSA'S
44 Province St
Downtown ②
+1 617 357 6861
samlagrassas.com

A favorite among Boston's downtown workers, Sam LaGrassa's is known for its hearty, towering pastrami and corned beef sandwiches, made with top-quality meats and fresh ingredients. The bustling lunchtime spot offers a casual setting, perfect for an affordable and satisfying midday meal that keeps locals coming back for more.

27 MONICA'S MERCATO & SALUMERIA

27 **ITALIAN SANDWICH**
AT: MONICA'S MERCATO & SALUMERIA
130 Salem St
North End ③
+1 617 742 4101
monicasnorthend.com

Don't let the line outside Monica's fool you, it's well worth the wait. Known for its hefty, flavorful Italian sandwiches filled with high-quality meats and fresh vegetables, this beloved spot delivers every time. Afterward, stroll a few blocks to the Greenway and enjoy your meal on what was once an aboveground highway.

28 **BANH MI**
AT: BA LE
1052 Dorchester Avenue
Dorchester ⑧
+1 617 265 7171
balebanhmiboston.com

Ba Le is a Vietnamese grocery store stocked with favorite Vietnamese snacks and baked goods. Most importantly, it is known to have the freshest *banh mi* in town. Each *banh mi* is made to order with deliciously flaky, freshly baked buns, and is even better when paired with a refreshing Vietnamese iced coffee.

29 **JOHN GOUDA-MAN CREPE**
AT: PARIS CREPERIE
278 Harvard St
Coolidge Corner ⑦
+1 617 232 1770
pariscreperie.com

Paris Creperie offers both sweet and savory crepes in the heart of Coolidge Corner, but the winner is the John Gouda-Man crepe, packed with smoked turkey and gooey Gouda cheese. This unassuming spot is perfect for a quick lunch before browsing the nearby bookshops and vintage stores.

30 **LAMB GYRO**
AT: GRECO
225 Newbury St
Back Bay ①
+1 617 589 1178
grecotrulygreek.com

At Greco, you can enjoy classic gyro wraps brimming with fresh ingredients tucked into warm, soft pita bread. The crowd favorite is the tender lamb gyro, stuffed with traditional ingredients, including hand-cut fries. Don't miss the crispy zucchini chips with tangy tzatziki sauce.

5 VEGETARIAN and VEGAN eateries

31 **LULU GREEN**
246 W Broadway
South Boston ⑤
+1 617 420 4070
lulugreen.com

Lulu Green is a chic, plant-based restaurant emphasizing seasonal, locally sourced ingredients. Although entirely vegetarian and vegan, you won't miss meat or cheese; their flavorful alternatives, such as seitan asada brunch tacos or dinner mezze with house-made cashew cheese, are just as delicious.

32 **VEGGIE GRILL**
57 John F. Kennedy St
Harvard Square ⑨
+1 617 275 8909
veggiegrill.com/location/veggie-grill-harvard-square

Veggie Grill, North America's leading plant-based restaurant chain, offers a menu full of hearty, responsibly sourced comfort foods like cheeseburgers and buffalo chicken wraps. It's the ideal fast food alternative for vegetarians and vegans; healthy, delicious, and satisfying without compromising on flavor.

33 **REDWHITE BONELESS RAMEN**
294 Newbury St
Back Bay ①
+1 857 277 0609
redwhiteusa.com

For a hearty, plant-based ramen, this is the go-to spot. Alongside its diverse ramen options, this Japanese eatery also serves plant-based avocado sushi. With a focus on healthy, high-quality ingredients, it shows that vegan food can be both flavorful and satisfying.

34 **PINK CARROT**
115 Salem St
North End ③
+1 857 233 5206
pinkcarrotboston.com

Amid Boston's Italian-centric North End, Pink Carrot offers a bold, colorful escape with its playful pink interior and focus on vegan and vegetarian dishes. The menu is packed with flavorful wraps, fresh salads, and juices, adding a healthy, refreshing alternative to the neighborhood's traditional dining options.

35 **CLOVER FOOD LAB**
496 Massachusetts Avenue
Harvard Square ⑨
+1 617 758 8550
cloverfoodlab.com

Once a popular food truck known for its chickpea wraps, Clover has evolved into a top destination for vegetarian and vegan cuisine. With a concise and flavorful menu that emphasizes fresh, locally sourced ingredients, Clover offers a relaxed lunch setting. Its commitment to sustainability sets it apart in the local dining scene.

34 PINK CARROT

5
FOOD INTOLERANCE FRIENDLY *destinations*

36 **VERVEINE CAFE & BAKERY**
298 Massachusetts Avenue
Central Square ⑨
+1 617 395 3125
verveinecafe.com

Verveine in Boston stands out with its entirely gluten-free menu, catering to everyone without compromise. Co-founder Monica Glass is celiac and Ken Oringer's daughter Verveine (the cafe's namesake) also has celiac disease. The delicious baked goods, pastries, and lunch offerings draw crowds, proving that gluten-free can be irresistible.

36 VERVEINE CAFE & BAKERY

37 **FACCIA A FACCIA**

278 Newbury St
Back Bay ①
+1 857 991 1080
facciabruttaboston.com

Faccia a Faccia is a coastal Italian restaurant that offers a safe and delicious dining experience with seasonal dishes. The menu features celiac-safe, housemade pasta and clearly labeled gluten-free options. The unpretentious atmosphere and meticulous attention to allergy concerns ensure a relaxed and enjoyable meal.

38 **CAROLICIOUS**

AT: AERONAUT BREWING COMPANY
14 Tyler St
Porter Square ⑩
+1 857 316 7842
carolicious.net

Carolicious serves traditional Venezuelan arepas with a New England twist. Everything on the menu is gluten-free, with vegan and vegetarian options available. Made from corn flour and served roasted, these healthy, flavorful arepas are a safe and delicious choice. It's a lively spot for great food and beer.

39 **LIFE ALIVE ORGANIC CAFE**

505 Tremont St
South End ①
+1 617 982 6633
lifealive.com

Life Alive is a welcoming space with a focus on organic whole foods. The menu features gluten-free, dairy-free, and vegan options, including delicious salad and grain bowls, smoothies, and juices. Connected to Down Under Yoga, it's an ideal spot to relax, recharge, and enjoy nutritious meals.

40 **POKE BY LOVE ART**

103 Beverly St
West End ②
+1 617 588 0889
loveartpoke.com

POKE by Love Art serves fresh, healthy, 100% gluten-free poke bowls. Customers can choose from curated bowls or create their own, with vegan and dairy-free options available. This Hawaiian-inspired eatery offering umami flavors is a top choice for takeout.

5 PIZZA SLICES
for every mood

41 **GALLERIA UMBERTO**
289 Hanover St
North End ③
+1 617 227 5709
@galleriaumberto

Galleria Umberto is a no-frills, old-school pizza experience in the heart of Boston. This cash-only spot operates out of a small, simple storefront and is renowned for its Sicilian-style pizza slices featuring generous square slices with thick, melty cheese and simple toppings. Get there early to avoid long lines.

42 **BREWER'S FORK**
7 Moulton St
Charlestown ④
+1 617 337 5703
brewersfork.com

Brewer's Fork serves up delicious artisanal wood-fired pizzas with gourmet toppings like spicy clam or sausage with fresh ricotta, atop a perfectly charred crust. The pizzeria's cozy industrial atmosphere and inviting patio are enhanced by an impressive selection of rotating draft beers, ideal for pairing with pizza.

43 **AVENUE KITCHEN + BAR**
158 Boston Avenue
Davis Square ⑩
+1 617 764 0879
avenuesomerville.com

Head to this cozy neighborhood joint for Detroit-style pizza; thick, crispy, cheese-crusted slices with a satisfyingly crunchy bottom. Chef Kenny, who's honed his craft in Michelin-starred and James Beard award-winning kitchens, elevates comfort food with delicious pizza and creative bar bites.

44 PRAIRIE FIRE

242 Harvard St
Coolidge Corner ⑦
+1 617 396 8199
prairiefirebrookline.com

Prairie Fire in Coolidge Corner serves wood-fired pizzas and vegetables, as well as fresh pastas. Featuring an expansive beer garden, it's the perfect spot to relax and enjoy delicious wood-fired cuisine and beer during warmer months. When it's too cold for the outdoor patio, the dark, wood-accented interior offers a warm, romantic setting.

45 SANTARPIO'S

111 Chelsea St
East Boston ⑥
+1 617 567 9871
santarpiospizza.com

Founded as a bakery in 1903 by an Italian immigrant, Santarpio's began selling pizza in 1930 and remains family-owned. While its exterior may not impress, inside you'll find simple, delicious pizzas with perfectly crispy crusts, considered by many as Boston's best. Many travelers have a tradition to stop here on their way to the airport.

42 BREWER'S FORK

The 5 freshest SEAFOOD spots

46 **OSTRA**
1 Charles St South
Back Bay ①
+1 617 421 1200
ostraboston.com

Drawing inspiration from both local and European cuisine, Ostra's menu features innovative and classic seafood dishes lightly cooked to enhance their natural flavors. The upscale yet elegantly simple setting showcases black-and-white oceanic photographs and fresh fish displayed on ice. The standout meal is a perfectly executed seafood paella made in the traditional Valencian style.

49 JAMES HOOK & CO.

47 **ATLANTIC FISH COMPANY**

761 Boylston St
Back Bay ①
+1 617 267 4000
atlanticfish.com

Atlantic Fish Company, a Boston staple, is renowned for its fresh, high-quality seafood sourced from a local family business dating back to 1906. The menu changes daily based on the morning's harbor catches, alongside classic New England dishes like lobster and clam chowder in a welcoming atmosphere.

48 **ROW 34**

383 Congress St
Seaport ⑤
+1 617 553 5900
row34.com

Housed in a renovated 1908 textile warehouse, Row 34 delivers a sleek, modern-industrial vibe. Known for its impressive raw bar featuring locally sourced oysters, the restaurant also boasts a well-curated craft beer selection. In addition to the dining room, there is also bar seating and a heated three-season patio.

49 **JAMES HOOK & CO.**

440 Atlantic Avenue
Waterfront ③
+1 617 423 5501
jameshooklobster.com

Since 1925, James Hook & Co. has been a staple on Boston's waterfront, famous for its fresh lobster rolls – best enjoyed cold for maximum flavor. This historic, rustic spot also serves seafood classics like lobster salad and chowder, offering a quintessential New England experience.

50 **SALTIE GIRL**

279 Dartmouth St
Back Bay ①
+1 617 267 0691
saltiegirl.com

Saltie Girl boasts a playful, colorful interior and a stylish patio. The menu stands out with offerings like tinned fish and caviar, enhanced by a charming mermaid-tiled bar. While each seafood and raw bar dish is uniquely presented, the standout is undoubtedly the fried lobster and waffles.

5 BOSTON INSTITUTIONS
worth the hype

51 **OLEANA**
134 Hampshire St
Mid-Cambridge ⑨
+1 617 661 0505
oleanarestaurant.com

Guided by Chef Ana Sortun, Oleana in Boston highlights Turkish and Middle Eastern cuisine with locally sourced ingredients. The intimate, elegant atmosphere and flavorful small plates make reservations highly sought after. Desserts, especially the famed baked Alaska, offer a memorable finish, capping off an already exceptional dining experience rooted in rich, aromatic flavors.

52 **EASTERN STANDARD KITCHEN AND DRINKS**
775 Beacon St
Fenway ⑦
+1 617 530 1590
easternstandard boston.com

Eastern Standard, a beloved brasserie near Fenway Park, serves a seamless blend of American and European-inspired dishes alongside a renowned cocktail list. After a brief closure, it has reopened just steps from its original location, drawing diners back with its welcoming atmosphere and consistently high-quality food.

53 O YA

9 East St
Chinatown ②
+1 617 654 9900
o-ya.restaurant

Since 2007, o ya has been one of Boston's most sought-after dining spots, known for its inventive Japanese-inspired *omakase*. With a cozy, 30-seat setting, it features a 20-course tasting menu blending traditional sushi techniques with bold flavors. Reservations remain tough to secure, reflecting its lasting allure in the city's dining scene

54 TORO

1704 Washington St
South End ①
+1 617 536 4300
toro-restaurant.com

Toro, located in the vibrant South End, serves up an impressive menu of Spanish tapas. Acclaimed chef Ken Oringer crafts authentic and inventive small plates in a bustling, rustic atmosphere. Toro also hosts an annual 'Running of the Bulls' event featuring wine from *porróns*, a parade of exceptional tapas, and a festive atmosphere.

55 NEPTUNE OYSTER

63 Salem St
North End ③
+1 617 742 3474
neptuneoyster.com

A line around the block is common at Neptune Oyster, renowned for its fresh seafood and decadent, buttery lobster rolls. This intimate, high-end eatery serves top-quality seafood in a cozy, classic setting with communal tables. While the price may be steep, the exceptional flavors and ingredients make it well worth the splurge.

5 COZY DISHES
for a chilly day

56 **RISOTTO**
AT: SRV
569 Columbus Avenue
South End ①
+1 617 536 9500
srvboston.com

SRV serves a luxurious, made-to-order risotto that's perfect for cozying up and savoring. With seasonal variations like squid ink, lobster, and truffles, this creamy dish caters to both vegetarians and non-vegetarians. Each bowl is a rich, comforting blend of indulgence and flavor, showcasing SRV's modern interpretation of traditional Venetian cuisine.

57 **POLLO PARMIGIANA**
AT: RINO'S PLACE
258 Saratoga St
East Boston ⑥
+1 617 567 7412
rinosplace.com

This old-school Italian establishment serves a hearty chicken parmesan that's the ultimate comfort dish. The portion is massive, covering the entire plate, with fork-tender chicken smothered in rich red sauce and paired with a side of homemade pasta. It's like enjoying a Sunday dinner at Nonna's, perfect for sharing or indulging solo.

58 **TABLESIDE BAKED POTATO**

AT: ABE & LOUIE'S

793 Boylston St

Back Bay ①

+1 617 536 6300

abeandlouies.com

At Abe & Louie's, the Tableside Baked Potato is a satisfying dish, prepared freshly tableside with sour cream, chives, bacon, and cheese, making it a hearty complement to their renowned steaks. For an even more indulgent twist, order the Million Dollar Baked Potato, topped with Kaluga caviar and smoked-sturgeon crème fraîche.

59 **STEAK TIPS**

AT: THE TIP TAP ROOM

138 Cambridge St

Beacon Hill ②

+1 857 350 3344

thetiptaproom.com

At The Tip Tap Room, the marinated and perfectly grilled steak tips are the standout dish, embodying high-end cuisine in a casual setting. Despite its bustling bar scene, patrons are drawn to these juicy tips served with creamy horseradish potatoes and rich bordelaise sauce – a hearty plate that showcases the restaurant's dedication to flavor.

60 **MAC N' CHEESE**

AT: SWEET CHEEKS Q

1381 Boylston St

Fenway ⑦

+1 617 266 1300

sweetcheeksq.com

Sweet Cheeks, a relaxed Fenway favorite by Top Chef finalist Tiffani Faison, embodies Southern hospitality with its soul-warming mac and cheese and Southern-inspired barbecue. The perfectly creamy mac and cheese, topped with crispy breadcrumbs, complements the barbecued meats and captures the comfort of Sunday dinners and backyard BBQs.

61 UNION OYSTER HOUSE

5 restaurants woven with HISTORY

61 **UNION OYSTER HOUSE**

41 Union St
Downtown ②
+1 617 227 2750
unionoysterhouse.com

As America's oldest continuously operating restaurant and oyster bar, open since 1826, Union Oyster House occupies Boston's oldest Georgian brick building. Located on the Freedom Trail, this historic landmark has served patrons like Daniel Webster and John F. Kennedy, offering a taste of history with its famed clam chowder and variously prepared oysters.

62 **HARVEST RESTAURANT**

44 Brattle St
Harvard Square ⑨
+1 617 868 2255
harvestcambridge.com

Harvest Restaurant, a Harvard Square staple since 1975, has been a pioneer in farm-to-table dining. Known for its innovative cuisine and cozy, elegant setting, it has a special place in culinary history as a favorite of Julia Child, who often dined here and inspired its commitment to celebrating New England's seasonal bounty.

63 **PARKER'S RESTAURANT**

AT: OMNI PARKER HOUSE

60 School St

Downtown ②

+1 617 725 1600

omnihotels.com/hotels/boston-parker-house/dining/parkers-restaurant

Established in 1855, Parker's Restaurant is the birthplace of the iconic Boston Cream Pie and Parker House Rolls. This historic venue has welcomed literary figures like Dickens and Thoreau, while legends suggest Ho Chi Minh worked as a baker and Malcolm X as a busboy, cementing its status as a treasured piece of Boston's history.

64 **MAMMA MARIA**

3 North Square

North End ③

+1 617 523 0077

mammamaria.com

Mamma Maria offers white-tablecloth Italian dining in the North End, featuring homemade pasta and standout dishes like rabbit ragu and beef carpaccio with black truffles. Overlooking historic North Square, the oldest public square in America, its elegant atmosphere and scenic views complement the area's deep historical charm.

65 **MR. BARTLEY'S BURGER COTTAGE**

1246 Massachusetts Avenue

Harvard Square ⑨

+1 617 354 6559

mrbartley.com

Since 1960, Mr. Bartley's has been a Harvard Square icon, transformed by Joe and Joan Bartley from a convenience store into a burger destination. Famous for its fresh, made-to-order burgers and quirky atmosphere, with specialty burgers named after pop culture icons, it has attracted locals and celebrities like Johnny Cash and Al Pacino.

5 *savory* SMALL PLATES *locales*

66 **FIELD & VINE**
9 Sanborn Court
Union Square ⑩
+1 617 718 2333
fieldandvine somerville.com

Field & Vine provides a communal yet romantic dining experience centered on ever-changing seasonal small plates. The plant-filled dining area complements their farm-to-table approach, highlighting fresh, local ingredients. Each beautifully plated dish offers unique flavors and abundant vegetarian options, adorned with whimsical touches of colorful flowers and herbs.

67 **SARMA**
249 Pearl St
Somerville ⑩
+1 617 764 4464
sarmarestaurant.com

Sarma delivers a modern twist on Middle Eastern small plates in a cozy, colorful space adorned with ceramics and mosaic lanterns. The menu features a diverse selection of Mediterranean meze inspired by the chef's travels, all made with fresh, seasonal ingredients. Perfect for sharing, it's an ideal way to explore the vast menu.

68 **MAHANIYOM**
236 Washington St
Brookline ⑦
+1 617 487 5986
mahaniyomboston.com

Mahaniyom offers an intimate dining experience, guiding guests through a flavorful journey of Thai cuisine. Focused on bold, authentic flavors, the tapas-style menu encourages exploration with dishes like crispy chicken skin, beef *massaman*, and crab fried rice. Each small plate reflects the restaurant's dedication to showcasing the depth of Thai flavors.

69 **MOONA**
243 Hampshire St
Inman Square ⑨
+1 617 945 7448
moonarestaurant.com

Moona showcases vibrant Mediterranean small plates inspired by Levantine traditions. In an intimate, mosaic-tiled setting, dishes like *za'atar*-crusted lamb and grilled halloumi are prepared with fresh, locally sourced ingredients. The menu highlights the flavors of the Arabic pantry, featuring seasonal produce and housemade spices, jams, and pickles, all available for purchase.

70 **LITTLE DONKEY**
505 Massachusetts Avenue
Central Square ⑨
+1 617 945 1008
littledonkeycambridge.com

Little Donkey's ever-evolving menu captures the essence of global cuisine, inspired by the chefs' extensive travels. It's the ideal spot for a night out with friends, offering something for every palate. Whether you're craving a familiar favorite or seeking something new, you'll find a dish that's both memorable and satisfying in this diverse culinary haven.

5 *hotspots for* LATIN AMERICAN *flavors*

71 **CHIVO TAQUERIA**
1728 Massachusetts Avenue
Porter Square ⑩
+1 857 242 3343
chivoboston.com

Bringing the bold flavors of Mexico and El Salvador to Cambridge, Chivo Taqueria offers authentic tacos, burritos, pupusas, and quesadillas. It stands out for its homemade tortillas and perfectly toasted burritos, and each meal is made with fresh ingredients and customizable toppings, served in generous portions.

72 **EL PEÑOL**
54 Bennington St
East Boston ⑥
+1 617 569 0100
elpenoleastboston.com

El Peñol in East Boston is a beloved spot for authentic Colombian cuisine, serving hearty dishes like *bandeja* and *sancocho de res*. Opened in 1998 by Colombian-born Marina Balvin, this welcoming restaurant offers a homelike atmosphere with delicious, flavorful food, friendly service, and a deep connection to Colombia's rich culinary traditions.

73 **CELESTE**

21 Bow St
Union Square ⑩
+1 617 616 5319
celesteunionsquare.com

Celeste is a Peruvian gem known for its ceviche and seafood dishes. The owners first gained notoriety for their intimate dinner parties, inspiring this cozy, welcoming restaurant. With fresh ingredients, aromatic spices, and dishes meant to be shared, Celeste captures the essence of Peru, making every meal feel like a special gathering.

74 **OLIVEIRA'S STEAK HOUSE**

120 Washington St
Somerville ⑨
+1 617 764 0455
oliveirassomerville.com

At Oliveira's Steak House, diners are treated to an authentic Brazilian *churrasco* experience, where a parade of *rodízio*-style meats is served directly at your table. With perfectly grilled cuts like sirloin and strip loin, a fresh buffet, and an energetic, welcoming atmosphere, this steakhouse captures the generous spirit of Brazil at an affordable price.

75 **ORINOCO**

22 Harvard St
Brookline ⑦
+1 617 232 9505
orinocokitchen.com

Orinoco, inspired by traditional Venezuelan *taguaritas*, is a cozy neighborhood spot serving family recipes in a warm, inviting atmosphere. Offering empanadas, arepas, and *pabellón criollo* – Venezuela's most folkloric dish – it brings the rich flavors of Latin America to life, using fresh, locally sourced ingredients that elevate the flavors of each dish.

5 must-try places for authentic
ASIAN CUISINE

76 **DYNASTY**
14-A Hudson St
Chinatown ②
+1 617 603 8796
dynastyboston.com

A recent addition to Boston's Chinatown, Dynasty has quickly garnered praise for its fresh, made-to-order dim sum. The extensive menu features traditional favorites like expertly prepared Peking duck, crafted with authentic techniques. Perfect for both dim sum enthusiasts and newcomers, the menu is easy to navigate with helpful pictures for guidance.

77 **BAB AL-YEMEN RESTAURANT**
468 Commonwealth Avenue
Fenway ⑦
+1 857 250 2943
babalyemenboston.com

Bringing the flavors of Yemen to Boston, Bab Al-Yemen Restaurant serves authentic meaty dishes like *lamb mandi* and *fahsah* stew. The dining space blends tradition and comfort, offering floor seating with patterned cushions and mosaic tables, alongside more conventional Western seating with chairs.

78 **YUME GA ARUKARA**
AT: LESLY UNIVERSITY PORTER SQUARE CAMPUS
1815 Massachusetts Avenue
Porter Square ⑩
yumegaarukara.com

Famous for its authentic cold Japanese udon, this unassuming restaurant serves both hot and cold udon with rich flavorful broths and housemade noodles, capturing the essence of Japanese comfort food. After finishing your bowl, staff invite you to make a wish, or simply enjoy a 'good job'.

79 **FUGAKYU**
1280 Beacon St
Coolidge Corner ⑦
+1 617 738 1268
fugakyu-brookline.com

FuGaKyu blends modern and traditional elements to deliver authentic Japanese dining with a wide selection of fresh sushi, sashimi, and traditional Japanese dishes. Its tatami rooms provide a private dining experience, while the intimate sushi bar invites conversation with the chef.

80 **PHO LE RESTAURANT**
1356 Dorchester Avenue
Dorchester ⑧
+1 617 506 6294
pholedorchester.com

Known for its consistent quality, Pho Le is a standout among Boston's Vietnamese restaurants, offering classics like pho and grilled meat vermicelli. With over 30 years in the restaurant industry, the Lê family establishment has grown from a small noodle shop to a full-service restaurant showcasing dishes from across Vietnam.

5 *elegant*
EUROPEAN KITCHENS

81 **GIULIA**
1682 Massachusetts Avenue
Porter Square ⑩
+1 617 441 2800
giuliarestaurant.com

Giulia specializes in handmade pasta and seasonal antipasti, featuring a menu that evolves with the freshest ingredients. At the heart of the restaurant is the custom-built pasta table, crafted from reclaimed white oak, where fresh pasta is rolled each day and served family-style each night. Standouts include chicken liver crostini and wild boar ragu pappardelle.

82 **BALEIA**
264 E Berkeley St
South End ①
+1 617 505 3243
baleiaboston.com

Showcasing the flavors of Portugal, Baleia's seafood-forward menu includes standout dishes like piri piri oysters and salt cod *bolinhos*, alongside traditional desserts such as *pastéis de nata*. Paying homage to Portugal's Mediterranean coast and seafaring heritage, the bright, inviting space is adorned with lime-washed walls and a chandelier designed to evoke a fishing net.

83 **MISTRAL**

223 Columbus Avenue
Back Bay ①
+1 617 867 9300
mistralbistro.com

Blending French Mediterranean flavors, Mistral offers a refined menu with dishes like duck confit in an elegant setting. The space features arched windows, handpicked French pottery, and decor inspired by the Provence region in France. The menu focuses on fresh, seasonal ingredients, delivering a dining experience rooted in French culinary traditions.

84 **PRIMA**

10 City Square
Charlestown ④
+1 617 804 7400
primaboston.com

Prima is an Italian steakhouse known for its high-quality steaks and Italian-inspired dishes. The dining room is buzzing with energy, but for a quieter experience, the outdoor patio or romantic Rose Room, featuring a dedicated bar, are great options. Their brunch stands out with upscale steak and eggs and Italian twists on classics.

85 **TABERNA DE HARO**

999 Beacon St
Brookline ⑦
+1 617 277 8272
tabernaboston.com

Bringing a taste of Spain to Boston, Taberna de Haro is known for its authentic Spanish tapas and dishes like garlic shrimp and paella. The extensive, all-Spanish wine list, curated by former owner and Madrid-certified sommelier Deborah Hansen, sets it apart, offering rare finds and perfect pairings. The cozy space and sidewalk patio capture the warmth of Spanish hospitality.

5 NORTH END ITALIAN *treasures*

86 **CARMELINA'S**
307 Hanover St
North End ③
+1 617 742 0020
carmelinasboston.com

Carmelina's serves large portions of authentic, made-to-order comfort food, in a light and airy space with an open kitchen and family photos on the walls. In the summer, its retractable front walls allow for open-air dining along the always-busy Hanover Street.

87 **ARYA TRATTORIA**
253 Hanover St, 2nd Fl.
North End ③
+1 617 742 1276
aryatrattoria.com

Tucked away on the second floor above Hanover Street, Arya offers an intimate dining experience featuring hearty Italian dishes like osso buco and *frutti di mare fra diavolo*. With a welcoming atmosphere and expert wine pairings, chef and owner Massimo Tiberi has created a hidden gem that draws both locals and celebrities alike.

88 BRICCO PANETTERIA

241 Hanover St
North End ③
+1 617 248 9859
briccosalumeria.com/panetteria

Hidden in a quiet alley, Bricco Panetteria offers top-notch artisanal breads. From prosciutto-stuffed ciabatta to olive-oil soaked focaccia, each loaf is made using traditional methods. The bakery's old brick structure and underground entrance add a sense of adventure, and it's hard to resist buying a loaf once you catch a whiff of freshly baked bread.

89 LA FAMIGLIA GIORGIO'S RISTORANTE

112 Salem St
North End ③
+1 617 367 6711
lafamigliagiorgios.com

Known for its family-style portions and Roman-inspired cuisine, La Famiglia Giorgio's serves up hearty Italian classics like meaty bolognese, and housemade pasta. The cozy atmosphere, reminiscent of Nonna's kitchen, pairs with generous portions, ensuring plenty of leftovers. With a long menu and gluten-free options, it's a great spot for a family feast.

90 CAFFÉ VITTORIA

290-296 Hanover St
North End ③
+1 617 227 7606
caffevittoria.com

Known as Boston's first Italian cafe, Caffé Vittoria has been serving cappuccinos, *cioccolato caldo*, and cannoli since 1929. Its vintage decor includes rare espresso machines, giving the space an old-world feel. Hidden in the basement is the last smoking lounge in the city, with a harrowed history.

89 LA FAMIGLIA GIORGIO'S RISTORANTE

5 FOOD TRUCKS *and* STREET FOOD *flavors*

91 **NUBIAN MARKETS**
2565 Washington St
Dorchester ⑧
+1 617 608 4940
nubianmarkets.com

Serving as a community hub in Roxbury, Nubian Markets features a cafe, halal butcher, and grocery store, and offers African street food like jerk chicken and harissa lamb sandwiches. The market showcases local Black-owned brands, rare African ingredients, and celebrates the rich culinary traditions of the African diaspora.

92 **BUENAS**
AT: BOW MARKET
1 Bow Market Way
Union Square ⑩
buenas.co

Bringing innovative twists to South American empanadas, this Bow Market eatery features a rotating menu with flavors like buffalo cauliflower, sorta samosa, and guava with cheese. They also offer take-and-bake empanadas, sauces, and dough for home cooking. The high-quality dough ensures they're delicious whether enjoyed fresh or baked at home.

93 KOSHARI MAMA

585 Somerville Avenue
Porter Square ⑩
+1 617 229 9230
kosharimama.com

Run by a mother-daughter duo, Koshari Mama serves vegan Egyptian street food with *koshari* as its star – a flavorful mix of rice, lentils, pasta, chickpeas, and crispy onions, served with a variety of sauces. The restaurant began as a pop-up at farmers markets and now has its own space, helping bring traditional Egyptian flavors to Boston.

94 NACO TACO

297 Massachusetts Avenue
Central Square ⑨
+1 617 945 1548
nacocentral.com

Naco Taco serves made-from-scratch tacos, tortas, and sides with bold flavors like crispy pork belly and *elote*, the essentials of Mexican street food. Opened in 2015, the restaurant features a lively atmosphere with a spacious outdoor patio. Their food trucks bring the same fresh tortillas and inventive dishes to various Boston locations.

95 BOONNOON

161 Massachusetts Avenue
Arlington ⑩
+1 781 316 0059
boonnoonmarket.com

BoonNoon Market offers authentic Thai street food in a cozy, plant-filled space alongside specialty Thai goods. With flavorful dishes like *khao soi* and satay noodles, the small, focused menu is known for its bold, well-executed flavors. The warm, friendly staff adds to the inviting, homey atmosphere, creating a dining experience rooted in comfort and tradition.

5

CULTURAL FUSION

restaurants

96 **COMFORT KITCHEN**
611 Columbia Road
Dorchester ⑧
+1 617 329 6910
comfortkitchenbos.com

Comfort Kitchen creates unique plates inspired by the flavors and spices of the international spice trade, spanning from Asia to the Americas. As a Black-, women-, and immigrant-owned restaurant, the focus goes beyond showcasing diverse flavors – they're equally committed to treating their staff with respect and ensuring a supportive, inclusive work environment.

97 **MOONSHINE 152**
152 Dorchester Avenue
South Boston ⑤
+1 617 752 4191
moonshine152.com

Moonshine 152 blends American and Asian flavors into bold comfort dishes like scallion pancake quesadillas and party tots with kimchi butter and truffled teriyaki. Chef Mei's creative menu reflects her dynamic style, offering both small and sharing sizes. It's ideal for long, relaxed meals indoors or on the patio.

98 **NZUKO**
60 Howard St
Watertown ⑦
+1 617 744 6017
nzukowatertown.com

Nzuko blends Caribbean flavors with the Mediterranean diet's health benefits, offering dishes like jerk chicken gyros and plantain hummus. Caribbean-born chef Laurette Ndukwe focuses on healthy, flavorful cuisine in a warm, inviting atmosphere to make customers feel at home.

99 **MYERS + CHANG**
1145 Washington St
South End ①
+1 617 542 5200
myersandchang.com

With exceptional Asian fusion flavors, Myers + Chang, led by Joanne Chang, offers a vibrant dining experience in the South End. Adorned with playful decor and a striking red dragon window decal, dishes like tea-smoked pork ribs and sweet and sour Brussels sprouts make it ideal for an inventive dim sum brunch.

100 **THE ELEPHANT WALK**
1415 Washington St
South End ①
+1 617 247 1500
elephantwalkboston.com

Founded in 1991 by Longteine 'Nyep' de Monteiro, an immigrant from Cambodia, The Elephant Walk artfully blends Cambodian and French cuisine with dishes like Cambodian *rouleaux* and braised duck in soy-ginger tamarind juices. The menu offers a mix of traditional favorites and fusion dishes.

5 *creative scoops of*

ICE CREAM

101 **FAR OUT**
419 Harvard St
Coolidge Corner ⑦
+1 617 487 8102
farouticecream.com

Far Out brings a taste of New Zealand to Boston with creamy soft-serve ice cream blended with fresh fruit mix-ins. Choose from traditional berries like kookaberry and blueberries, or enjoy seasonal fruits like apples and cherries in the fall. This simple yet inventive approach allows for endless, customizable flavor combinations, including non-dairy options.

102 **NORTH END CREAMERY**
121 Salem St
North End ③
northendcreamery.com

North End Creamery stands out among gelato stands by offering homemade artisanal ice creams in unique flavors like taro, Thai tea coconut, and pistachio port wine. This charming, brightly colored shop prioritizes freshness and quality, making it the perfect stop for a delightful treat after exploring the bustling streets.

103 **TOSCANINI'S**
159 First St
Kendall Square ⑨
+1 617 491 5877
tosci.com

Toscanini's in Cambridge has long been celebrated for its inventive, high-quality flavors, like burnt caramel, goat cheese brownie, and B3 (brownie, brown butter, brown sugar). Using traditional slow-churning methods, this ice cream achieves an exceptionally creamy texture that's irresistible, so be sure to grab a pint.

104 **FOMU**

655 Tremont St
South End ①
+1 617 982 7955
fomuicecream.com

FoMu Ice Cream redefines vegan desserts with its rich, coconut milk-base. Each small batch is creamy and indulgent, delivering full flavor without compromise. The menu includes signature flavors, limited-edition specials, and treats like ice-cream sandwiches, cakes, and frappes, ensuring everyone can enjoy its high-quality, plant-based offerings.

105 **HONEYCOMB CREAMERY**

1702 Massachusetts Avenue
Porter Square ⑩
+1 617 714 3983
honeycomb creamery.com

Although the Chaco Taco is retired, Honeycomb Creamery continues to indulge us with their own ice-cream tacos available exclusively on Taco Tuesdays. These tacos feature creamy ice cream in homemade shells and are served on a first-come, first-served basis. The shop also offers inventive, small-batch flavors made from local, seasonal ingredients.

101 **FAR OUT**

THE GREEN DRAGON TAVERN

70 PLACES FOR A DRINK

5 *cups of*

COFFEE FOR AFICIONADOS

106 **POUR OVER**

AT: RECREO COFFEE & ROASTERIE

1876 Centre St

West Roxbury ⑦

+1 617 553 2379

recreocoffee.com

Recreo Coffee specializes in single-origin Nicaraguan coffee from a family farm in Jinotega. Guests can savor freshly roasted pour-over coffee on a colorful patio or purchase beans to take home. The cafe's ambiance, with exposed brick walls and tin roofs, echoes South America, and the family-run coffee farm supports local families in Nicaragua.

106 RECREO COFFEE & ROASTERIE

107 **CORTADO**

AT: CURIO COFFEE

441 Cambridge St
East Cambridge ⑨
+1 857 242 3018
curiocoffee.com

Serving up expertly crafted cortados among other espresso drinks, Curio Coffee feels like a cafe straight out of Australia. This cozy spot, adorned with vintage charm, offers a perfect blend of rich espresso and velvety milk. Don't miss out on an accompanying freshly made waffle with your morning coffee.

108 **MOCHA**

AT: L.A. BURDICK

220 Clarendon St
Back Bay ①
+1 617 303 0113
burdickchocolate.com

L.A. Burdick may be known for its fine chocolates, but it also boasts one of the most indulgent espresso mochas in Boston. Diverging from the practice of using chocolate syrup, L.A. Burdick replaces syrup for pure melted fine chocolate: dark, milk or white.

109 **VIETNAMESE COFFEE**

AT: PHINISTA

96 Peterborough St
Fenway ⑦
+1 617 262 7700
phinista.com

Vietnamese coffee culture has a penchant for sweetening coffee with condensed milk. The Phinista Saigonese iced coffee celebrates this practice using traditional Vietnamese coffee, known for its robust flavor and strong brew, married with the velvety condensed milk, offering a sensory experience.

110 **CAPPUCCINO**

AT: THINKING CUP

236 Hanover St
North End ③
+1 857 233 5277
thinkingcup.com

Thinking Cup baristas showcase mastery in crafting a cappuccino - a harmonious blend of espresso and velvety milk, allowing the rich flavor of the Stumptown coffee beans to shine. Here, locals exchange morning news over their coffee, creating an authentic atmosphere that blends with the energetic buzz of tourists.

5 *delightful* CUPS OF TEA

111 **RITE TEA & ESPRESSO BAR**
525 Western Avenue
Allston ⑨
rite-tea-espresso-bar.square.site

Rite offers a range of tea and espresso drinks, including seasonal specialties like sweet pea matcha lattes. The sleek, purple bar sets the tone for this modern cafe, which provides an intimate setting perfect for gatherings, classes, and book clubs. Knowledgeable staff are passionate about tea and can assist in guiding undecided visitors.

112 **TEA BY THE SEA**
99 Sumner St
Retail Unit
East Boston ⑥
+1 508 685 7127
teabytheseaboston.com

Tea by the Sea, true to its name, offers a serene waterfront setting perfect to enjoy a wide variety of teas. Tea options include rich, creamy milk teas, refreshing fruit tea smoothies, and tea topped with traditional cheese foam, and each drink is customizable to your desired level of sweetness.

113 **MEM TEA**

196 Elm St
Davis Square ⑩
+1 617 627 9500
memteaimports.com

Established in 1999, MEM Tea is celebrated for its extensive selection of loose-leaf teas and expert in-house blending. Their commitment extends to educating both customers and businesses across New England on the intricacies of tea. Visitors can sip freshly brewed tea while exploring all of the tea options, all under the guidance of knowledgeable staff.

114 **OGAWA**

10 Milk St
Downtown ②
+1 617 780 7139
ogawacoffeeusa.com

Ogawa Coffee, a Japanese coffee shop, specializes in high-quality coffee and premium matcha sourced from Uji, Japan. The minimalist, modern cafe embodies Japanese aesthetics and a commitment to environmental responsibility. Skilled baristas focus on traditional preparation techniques, showcasing their artistry with beautifully presented latte art.

115 **TEN ONE TEA HOUSE**

279 Newbury St
Back Bay ①
+1 774 371 3195
tenoneteahouse.com

Specializing in healthy, creative boba tea, Ten One Tea House offers a variety of flavors and unique toppings. Originating from Taiwan, this shop prides itself on using simple, high-quality ingredients. Customize everything from the tea and boba flavor to sweetness levels. The store maintains a spotless environment, ensuring fresh boba at all times.

5 *local* **CIDER** *bars and taprooms*

116 **DOWNEAST CIDER HOUSE TAPROOM**
256 Marginal St
East Boston ⑥
+1 857 301 8881
downeastcider.com

Located on an industrial wharf in East Boston, Downeast Cider serves unfiltered, freshly pressed hard apple cider in a laid-back taproom. Visitors can sample innovative blends and seasonal offerings, like summer blueberry and fall pumpkin ciders, highlighting the brand's dedication to quality and a nod to its Maine roots.

117 **NIGHT SHIFT BREWING**
87 Santilli Hwy
Everett ⑩
+1 617 294 4233
nightshiftbrewing.com

Night Shift Brewing in Everett offers a diverse selection of inventive craft beers, from tangy sours to hoppy IPAs and rich stouts. The welcoming taproom, complete with live music and food trucks, along with Owl's Nest beer gardens across the city, provides a fun atmosphere for enjoying locally brewed favorites and unique experimental batches.

118 **SAM ADAMS BREWERY**

30 Germania St
Jamaica Plain ⑦
+1 617 368 5080
samadamsboston brewery.com

Sam Adams Brewery in Jamaica Plain offers an iconic brewing experience, highlighting its rich history in pioneering craft beers. Visitors can sample exclusive brews in the taproom, explore the brewing process, and delve into the brewery's storied past, gaining insight into the legacy of one of America's most influential breweries.

119 **LAMPLIGHTER BREWING CO.**

284 Broadway
Mid-Cambridge ⑨
+1 617 945 0450
lamplighter brewing.com

Lamplighter Brewing specializes in small-batch, experimental beers brewed with creativity and precision. The cozy taproom fosters a community vibe, inviting guests to enjoy board games while sampling their inventive brews. For those seeking a break from beer, they also offer freshly roasted coffee, providing a refreshing alternative or a perfect post-beer pick-me-up.

120 **TRILLIUM BREWING COMPANY**

50 Thomson Pl
Seaport ⑤
+1 857 449 0083
trilliumbrewing.com/pages/fort-point

Trillium Brewing is known for its New England-style IPAs and artisanal approach to brewing. The modern, industrial taproom in Fort Point provides a dynamic space with a roof deck and patio, ideal for enjoying their bold, high-quality beers. Weekly events like trivia and live music add to the engaging atmosphere.

5 pubs for a pint of GUINNESS

121 **IRISH VILLAGE**
224 Market St
Brighton ⑦
+1 617 787 5427
irishvillageboston.com/#about

Irish Village, established in 1970 by Irish immigrants, is a classic Irish pub known for its stately dark wood bar and warm brick and maroon decor. It's the ideal spot to enjoy a perfectly poured pint of Guinness, while the upbeat atmosphere, attracts a bustling and friendly local crowd.

122 **EIRE PUB**
795 Adams St
Dorchester ⑧
+1 617 436 0088
eirepub.com

Eire Pub embodies traditional Irish charm and a rich political legacy, having hosted Presidents Reagan and Clinton. With its expertly poured Guinness, this storied spot in Boston was initially a 'men's bar' and continues to be a magnet for political figures and local patrons alike.

123 **THE DRUID**
1357 Cambridge St
Inman Square ⑨
+1 617 497 0965
druidpub.com

Inside Cambridge's oldest wooden mercantile building, The Druid Bar offers a timeless atmosphere with traditional Irish music sessions. Alongside its perfect Guinness pour, the bar serves homemade Irish fare alongside American pub classics. With cozy, warm interiors decorated with old posters and photographs, it's a favorite haunt for locals.

124 PLOUGH AND THE STARS

912 Massachusetts Avenue
Central Square ⑨
+1 617 576 0032
ploughandstars.com

The Plough and the Stars, a neighborhood staple for over 50 years, blends the charm of a worn-in Irish pub with a vibrant music scene, echoing the community spirit of Dublin's pubs. Enjoy a perfectly poured Guinness while listening to live performances daily, featuring both emerging and established artists.

125 THE BLACK ROSE

160 State St
Downtown ②
+1 857 465 4100
blackroseboston.com

The Black Rose, an iconic Boston pub in Faneuil Hall since 1976, features daily live Celtic music that invites crowd participation. With expertly poured Guinness and traditional Irish fare, it attracts a mix of locals and visitors. Despite its central location, the pub maintains an authentic atmosphere, avoiding the typical tourist vibe.

124 PLOUGH AND THE STARS

5 *energetic*
SPORTS BARS

126 **PARLOR SPORTS**
1 Beacon St
Inman Square ⑨
+1 617 576 0231
@parlorsports

Parlor Sports in Somerville features a curved bar and ten strategically placed TVs, ensuring there are no bad seats. Unique touches like a vintage ringside-style bell and a drop-down boxing mic add character. Catering not just to sports fans, the bar hosts diverse watch parties, with its weekly schedule available on Instagram.

127 **BLEACHER BAR**
82A Lansdowne St
Fenway ⑦
+1 617 262 2424
bleacherbarboston.com

Located beneath Fenway Park's centerfield bleachers, Bleacher Bar offers a one-of-a-kind game-viewing experience at field level. Baseball fans can enjoy live action while savoring drinks and pub fare, all without a game ticket. Patrons are rotated for a prime view, ensuring everyone gets to enjoy the field, making each visit memorable.

128 THE BANSHEE

934 Dorchester Avenue
Dorchester ⑧
+1 617 436 9747
bansheeboston.com

The Banshee, Boston's go-to sports bar for live Premier League football and rugby, also covers a wide range of sports. Spanning two floors with numerous flat-screen TVs, it's known for its welcoming atmosphere and early openings, ensuring European fans catch their favorite matches without missing a beat.

129 STATS

77 Dorchester St
South Boston ⑤
+1 617 268 9300
statsboston.com

Stats is a spacious sports bar in South Boston, attracting a younger crowd, especially on big game days like Sunday night football. With 24 large screens, an extensive beer selection, and a sizable outdoor patio, it's a prime spot for enjoying live action with a fun, energetic crowd.

130 SULLIVAN'S TAP

168 Canal St
West End ②
sullivanstapboston.com

Opened in 1933, Sullivan's Tap is Boston's oldest sports bar, located just steps from TD Garden. It's a favorite spot for hockey and basketball fans to enjoy pregame drinks or catch the action on screen. Known for its cheap drinks, friendly service, and bar games, it creates the perfect game-day atmosphere.

5 places to
SIP THROUGH TIME

131 **WARREN TAVERN**
2 Pleasant St
Charlestown ④
+1 617 241 8142
warrentavern.com

Established in 1780 in Charlestown, Warren Tavern holds the distinction of being the oldest tavern in Massachusetts. Frequented by historical figures like Paul Revere and George Washington, the tavern's enduring colonial charm provides a unique backdrop for enjoying a fresh ale after exploring the Freedom Trail.

131 WARREN TAVERN

132 **GREEN DRAGON TAVERN**

11 Marshall St
Downtown ②
+1 617 367 0055
greendragon boston.com

The Green Dragon Tavern, established in 1654 and known as the 'Headquarters of the Revolution,' was once a gathering spot for figures like Paul Revere, playing a key role in planning aspects of the American Revolution. Today, it serves traditional pub fare in a setting that reflects its historic, revolutionary roots.

133 **AMRHEINS**

80 W Broadway
South Boston ⑤
+1 617 268 6189
amrheinsboston.com

Founded in 1890, Amrheins is the oldest bar in South Boston, boasting the oldest hand-carved bar in the country and reportedly the first draft beer pump in Boston. It offers traditional American and Italian fare, a rotating selection of draft beers, and is popular for its breakfast.

134 **LAST HURRAH**

AT: OMNI PARKER HOUSE
60 School St
Downtown ②
+1 617 305 1888
omnihotels.com/hotels/ boston-parker-house/ dining/the-last-hurrah

The Last Hurrah pays tribute to Boston's rich political history. Named after Edwin O'Connor's novel, the bar has hosted countless politicians and celebrities, including the iconic moment when JFK proposed to Jackie O and later announced his candidacy. With its refined decor and classic cocktails, it exudes timeless sophistication.

135 **SAIL LOFT**

80 Atlantic Avenue
Waterfront ③
+1 617 227 7280
thebostonsailloft.com

The Sail Loft in Boston has been a popular destination since the 1980s. Known for its nautical decor, it celebrates Boston's maritime history and serves as a casual spot for enjoying fresh seafood and drinks overlooking the harbor.

5 *intimate*

WINE BARS

136 **SPOKE WINE BAR**
89 Holland St
Davis Square ⑩
+1 617 718 9463
spokewinebar.com

Spoke Wine Bar offers an intimate and sophisticated atmosphere, perfect for a romantic date night. Their diverse selection of natural old-world wines from exceptional, lesser-known regions, pairs with beautifully composed small plates. With a seasonal menu and an ever-refreshing wine list, there's always something new to discover.

137 **GEORGIE'S WINE BAR**
100 Summer St
Downtown ②
+1 617 800 6189
georgieswine.com

Georgie's Wine Bar serves an extensive selection of global wines in a cozy, welcoming atmosphere. During the summer, the patio becomes a favorite spot for enjoying a relaxed evening with friends. Special weekly events like Midweek Mag(num) and Fine and Rare Friday give guests the chance to sample exclusive wines.

138 NATHALIE

186 Brookline Avenue
Fenway ⑦
+1 857 317 3884
nathaliebar.com

Nathalie spotlights small-production, natural wines from female winemakers worldwide, in a chic, modern setting with indoor and outdoor seating. Unique for offering half-bottle options without an upcharge, it encourages wine exploration, and its community-focused events like Brunch Jam sessions and LGBTQ+ Ladies Night make it welcoming and inclusive.

139 REBEL REBEL

1 Bow Market Way
Union Square ⑩
+1 617 721 7773
rebelrebelsomerville.com

Located in Bow Market, Rebel Rebel is a wine bar focused on natural wines and fostering community. Guests can enjoy their wine anywhere in the market courtyard, and regular events like wine classes and queer knitting circles add to its welcoming atmosphere, making it a great space for social connection.

140 TROQUET ON SOUTH

107 South St
Downtown ②
+1 617 695 9463
troquetboston.com

Troquet on South's wine list affirms its standing among Boston's top wine programs, guided by owner and sommelier Chris Campbell. In addition to a list of nearly a thousand bottles, there are impressive by-the-glass and flight options that can be paired with either a laid-back bar menu or a more formal dinner menu.

5 *bars with a* **VIEW**

141 **STRATUS BAR**
800 Boylston St, Floor 51
Back Bay ①
+1 617 544 3535
viewboston.com/stratus

Stratus Bar, perched atop the Prudential Center, has Boston's highest rooftop views, with sweeping city panoramas. It's perfect for sunset cocktails, featuring both indoor and outdoor seating. While the indoor space is inviting, the outdoor terrace truly shines on warmer days, offering unmatched views of the skyline and a relaxed atmosphere.

142 **LEGAL HARBORSIDE**
270 Northern Avenue
Seaport ⑤
+1 617 477 2900
legalseafoods.com/locations/boston-harborside

Legal Harborside boasts expansive views of East Boston and the harbor, with three distinct dining experiences. The casual first floor, refined second floor, and The Overlook, its newly renovated rooftop with a retractable roof, offer varied atmospheres for year-round drinks and seafood, making it ideal for everything from casual drinks to a full meal.

143 PIER 6

1 8th St
Charlestown ④
+1 617 337 0054
pier6boston.com

Pier 6 in Charlestown sits along the Boston Harbor with peaceful water views and panoramic vistas of the skyline. The upstairs dining room's floor-to-ceiling windows and the spacious outdoor deck provide ideal vantage points. Adding to the experience, you can also hear the sound of the USS *Constitution* cannon firing at sunset.

144 TALL SHIP

1 E Pier Dr
East Boston ⑥
+1 617 307 7714
tallshipboston.com

Tall Ship, a floating bar docked at Pier One in East Boston, is in a unique nautical setting with stunning harbor views. Guests can sip craft cocktails and enjoy fresh oysters aboard the 245-foot vessel, while the surrounding waterfront venue features live entertainment, food vendors, and outdoor games.

145 OVER THE CHARLES

400 Soldiers Field Rd
Allston ⑨
+1 617 222 0788
opentable.com/r/over-the-charles-boston-2

Over the Charles, atop the DoubleTree Hotel in Cambridge, offers 16th-floor views of the Charles River and Boston skyline. Open seasonally, this casual rooftop bar serves cocktails, local craft beers, and light bites. It's an often overlooked spot, but perfect for unwinding with a drink while taking in the serene river and city views.

5 *warm*

OUTDOOR PATIOS

146 **BOWERY BAR**
2261 Dorchester Avenue
Dorchester ⑧
+1 617 698 2261
bowery-bar.com

During the colder months, Bowery Bar in Dorchester transforms its spacious patio into a winter wonderland featuring heated outdoor yurts for a unique dining experience. While it's a local haunt in the summer, the winter yurts draw even more visitors who are willing to venture out to enjoy this special setting.

147 **PUBLICO STREET BISTRO & GARDEN**
11 Dorchester St
South Boston ⑤
+1 617 622 5700
publicoboston.com

Publico Street Bistro & Garden's European-style courtyard features heaters and a retractable roof, ideal for year-round outdoor dining. In winter, it transforms into a ski lodge, complete with fire pits and seasonal cocktails, creating a warm, festive atmosphere and instilling a bit of joy to the colder months.

148 **SHORT PATH DISTILLERY**

71 Kelvin St
Everett ⑩
+1 617 830 7954
shortpathdistillery.com

With a spacious, heated and covered patio, Short Path allows guests to enjoy its house-made spirits like small-batch rum and gin, and creative cocktails, even in colder months. Though the distillery doesn't serve food, guests are encouraged to bring their own or have food sent to the distillery, adding to its relaxed, open vibe.

149 **DAEDALUS RESTAURANT**

45 1/2 Mt Auburn St
Harvard Square ⑨
+1 617 349 0071
daedalusrestaurant cambridge.com

With a rooftop patio offering views over historic Harvard Square, Daedalus provides a cozy atmosphere with heaters for colder months. The menu focuses on modern American dishes with seasonal ingredients, while the bar serves a variety of cocktails and drinks, creating a comfortable space for enjoying food and drinks even in winter.

150 **ENVOY ROOFTOP**

70 Sleeper St
Seaport ⑤
+1 617 530 1538
envoyrooftop.com

Located at the edge of the Seaport District, Envoy Rooftop features a chic patio with sweeping views of the city and harbor. In winter, the space transforms with see-through igloos and specialty seasonal cocktails, creating a cozy escape. It's an ideal spot to take in the skyline while staying warm.

5 EXPERIENTIAL
bars and cafes

151 **KNIGHT MOVES CAFE**
1402 Beacon St
Coolidge Corner ⑦
+1 617 487 5259
knightmovescafe.com

Knight Moves Cafe is a board game lover's haven, featuring a vast collection of games for all ages. Regular game nights create the perfect setting for socializing, and while the cafe provides a limited selection of snacks and drinks, guests are encouraged to bring their own, enhancing its inviting vibe.

152 **CENTRAL PARK LANES**
10 Saratoga St
East Boston ⑥
+1 617 567 7073
@centralparklanes

Central Park Lanes offers a nostalgic experience with vintage candlepin bowling, a New England classic. Adding to the retro vibe, the lanes require manual scoring and resetting, and the bar is BYOB. Thursday league nights are perfect for people watching, but be prepared for limited availability of open lanes.

153 **ROXY'S ARCADE**
292 Massachusetts Avenue
Central Square ⑨
+1 617 714 4858
roxysarcade.com

A classic arcade meets cocktails and pub fare at Roxy's Arcade, where a wide selection of vintage games and pinball machines draws both enthusiasts and nostalgia seekers. Neon lights from the machines cast a colorful glow, amplifying the retro vibe.

154 **PKL BOSTON**

64 C St
South Boston ⑤
+1 617 315 7265
playpkl.com

The pickleball craze is still alive in Boston, and PKL Boston brings the excitement of pickleball indoors with year-round courts. The sports-focused venue is perfect for playing or watching pickleball while socializing with friends over drinks and food. The peak time to visit is during brunch, when bottomless mimosas add to the fun atmosphere.

155 **TAVERN OF TALES**

1478 Tremont St
Mission Hill ⑦
+1 617 708 0172
tavernoftales.com

Tavern of Tales offers an engaging board game experience with a wide selection of free games available, as well as reservable private rooms for more complex games. The venue hosts recurring events like Dungeons & Dragons and Magic the Gathering meet-ups, complemented by a menu of themed food and drinks to enjoy while you play.

152 **CENTRAL PARK LANES**

5 *imaginative* COCKTAIL BARS

156 **TEMPLE RECORDS**
17 Temple Pl
Downtown ②
+1 857 449 9003
templerecordsbar.com

Temple Records is a cozy, narrow bar inspired by 1950s Japanese listening bars, with walls lined with vinyl records, posters, and Japanese music memorabilia. Guests can enjoy an eclectic vinyl soundtrack while sipping on a selection of whiskeys, Japanese gins, sake, *shōchū*, and beers. Shaken cocktails are excluded to keep the focus on the classics.

157 **WUSONG ROAD**
112 Mt Auburn St
Harvard Square ⑨
+1 617 528 9125
wusongroad.com

Blending tiki bar vibes with Chinese-American tapas, Wusong Road in Cambridge's uniquely narrow Conductor's Building offers an exotic escape, even in winter. Adorned with tropical decor, jungle-inspired bars, and a replica of a Balinese temple door, it serves creative cocktails in beautifully crafted, original tiki mugs that are also available for purchase.

158 **FARMACIA**
5 N Square
North End ③
farmacianorthend.com

No visit to Farmacia is ever the same due to its ever-changing cocktail menu. With only nine seats, reservations are highly sought after. Every few months, a new theme showcases a concise cocktail menu inspired by regional and cultural influences, complete with themed music and ambiance. Every experience includes four cocktails and accompanying snacks.

159 **BARLETTE**
318 Harvard St
Coolidge Corner ⑦
+1 601 301 2024
drinkatbarlette.com

Barlette occupies a space reminiscent of a chic New York City apartment, with themed nooks, dramatic floral accents, and a cozy ambience – perfect for a stylish and comfortable night with friends without the hassle of cleanup. Cocktails feature fresh, seasonal mixers that rotate throughout the year, as well as beloved classics.

160 **HECATE**
48 Gloucester St
Back Bay ①
hecatebar.com

Hecate Bar will immerse you in a mystical experience inspired by the goddess of magic and transformation. The menu, crafted as a book of 'rites and rituals,' features inventive cocktails made with high-quality ingredients. This intimate, dimly lit speakeasy, accessed through an alley, offers a unique atmosphere with delicious cocktails and a skilled, knowledgeable staff.

5 SPEAKEASIES and JAZZ BARS

161 **WIG SHOP BOSTON**
27 Temple Pl
Downtown ②
+1 617 338 6333
wigshopboston.com

Wig Shop Boston stands out with its playful speakeasy ambiance and imaginative cocktail creations. The bar's quirky decor pays homage to its history as a wig shop, featuring mini wigs on liquor bottles and vintage wig advertisements. Creative Prohibition-era-inspired drinks, topped with whimsical garnishes like glitter foam and cotton candy, enhance the experience.

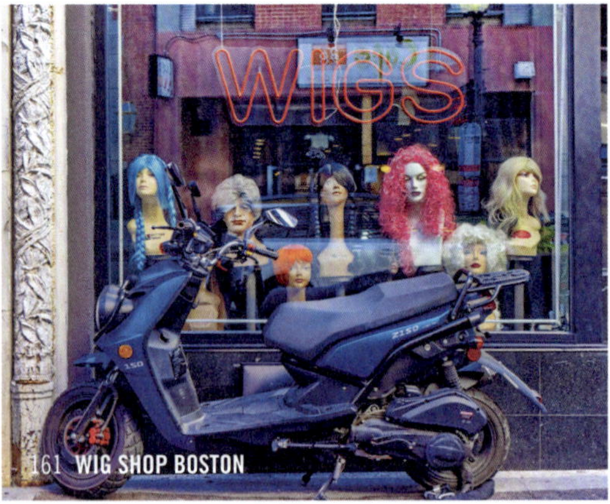

161 WIG SHOP BOSTON

162 **WALLY'S CAFE**
427 Massachusetts Avenue
Roxbury ①
+1 617 828 1754
wallyscafe.com

Wally's Cafe, Boston's oldest and New England's first Black-owned jazz club, has been a local icon since 1947. With an intimate setting and nightly performances, it has hosted legends like Billie Holiday and Charlie Parker, and continues to provide a genuine jazz experience while showcasing diverse talent.

163 **YVONNE'S**
2 Winter Pl
Downtown ②
+1 617 267 0047
yvonnesboston.com

Hidden behind a faux hair salon where the historic Locke-Ober restaurant once stood, Yvonne's is a chic speakeasy and modern supper club in Boston. It merges old-world elegance with a contemporary twist, offering globally inspired dishes and creative cocktails.

164 **BACKBAR**
7 Sanborn Ct
Union Square ⑩
backbarunion.com

Behind a discreet entrance, Backbar is a hidden haven for cocktail lovers. Its modest exterior conceals skilled bartenders who craft inventive, seasonal drinks customized to your taste. With its pop culture-inspired cocktails and laid-back vibe, Backbar offers a refreshingly inclusive atmosphere, without the usual influencer crowd.

165 **BEEHIVE**
541 Tremont St
South End ①
+1 617 423 0069
beehiveboston.com

The Beehive hosts soulful jazz brunches and nightly live music spanning various genres. In the vibrant South End, this underground venue exudes bohemian charm with eclectic decor and lively performances. Whether for cocktails or dinner, the music elevates every visit.

The 5 hippest DIVE BARS

166 **THE QUIET FEW**
331 Sumner St
East Boston ⑥
+1 617 561 1061
thequietfew.com

The Quiet Few is a relaxed dive bar with a friendly, unpretentious vibe, featuring an extensive whiskey selection and excellent food. The staff, including the owner who might be behind the bar or clearing tables, are attentive and welcoming. Don't let the casual atmosphere fool you, the drinks and food are worth it.

167 **BIDDY EARLY'S**
141 Pearl St
Downtown ②
+1 617 654 9944
biddyearlysboston.com

Biddy Early's is Boston's quintessential dive bar, tucked away in a basement with cheap beers and an old school retro vibe. It's the perfect spot to unwind with friends, whether you're enjoying a casual drink, engaging in lively conversation, or challenging each other to a few rounds of darts.

168 J.J. FOLEY'S

117 E Berkeley St
South End ①
+1 617 728 9101
jjfoleyscafe.com

Founded in 1909, J.J. Foley's is a historic dive bar that captures the essence of a classic Irish pub. Known for its traditional Irish fare and extensive beer selection, this family-owned establishment has been a fixture of Boston bar culture for over a century.

169 THE TAM

222 Tremont St
Chinatown ②
+1 857 277 0636
thetamboston.com

The Tam has been exuding cozy, unpretentious vibes since the 1940s. This iconic watering hole in the Theater District is known for its no-nonsense, cash-only approach, attracting a diverse crowd seeking affordable drinks and a welcoming atmosphere before enjoying a comedy show or concert nearby.

170 BUKOWSKI TAVERN

50 Dalton St
Back Bay ①
+1 617 437 9999
bukowski-tavern.com

Built beneath a parking garage, Bukowski Tavern delivers a low-key dive bar experience with an ever-changing lineup of twenty draft beers and satisfying comfort food. Its offbeat decor and casual atmosphere create a refreshing escape from the hustle of Newbury and Boylston Streets, attracting regulars who enjoy its quirky vibe and beer offerings.

5 HOOKAH *and* SMOKE LOUNGES

171 **S&A CIGARS**
52 Mt Auburn St
Watertown ⑦
+1 617 923 2111
cigargod.com

S&A Cigars, run by a friendly father-son team, attracts regulars with its extensive selection of cigars, including rare and hard-to-find options. The shop also features a cozy lounge with a poker table and TV, offering a relaxed, comfortable space where smokers can unwind and enjoy their cigars.

172 **APEX NOIRE**
150 State St
Downtown ②
+1 857 772 7164
apexnoire.com/Downtown

Set in the heart of Faneuil Hall, Apex Noire transforms the cannabis experience as Boston's first experiential dispensary with a bar. The unique top-floor bar offers a laid-back atmosphere with great music and drinks. Friendly and knowledgeable staff help customers navigate its bountiful and varied inventory.

173 **STANZA DEI SIGARI**
292 Hanover St
North End ③
+1 617 227 0295
stanzadeisigari.com/NorthEnd

Housed in a former 1920s speakeasy beneath Boston's North End, Stanza Dei Sigari exudes old-world charm with premium cigars and spirits. Marked by a large smoking stogie above the door, its dimly lit interior features cozy booths, a full bar, and an extensive selection of liquors.

174 **HABIBI'S LOUNGE**

1217 Commonwealth Avenue
Allston ⑨
+1 617 955 -2064
habibislounge.com

Habibi's Lounge, opened by a Lebanese student, offers flavorful tobaccos, Middle Eastern snacks, and sweet tea. Guests can unwind on cushioned couches around handmade mosaic tables as traditional Arabic music plays. The relaxed atmosphere and welcoming service make it a favorite spot for enjoying hookah.

175 **ANDALA COFFEE HOUSE**

286 Franklin St
Central Square ⑨
+1 617 945 2212
andalacoffee.com

Tucked away on a quiet street, Andala Coffee House has a cozy, Jerusalem-inspired atmosphere in an 18th-century residence. Fresh coffee, delicious Middle Eastern snacks and hookahs are available on the charming vine-covered patio or inside the welcoming cafe, making it a popular space for study sessions and casual gatherings.

172 **APEX NOIRE**

NARRATIVE

60 PLACES TO SHOP

5
INDEPENDENT BOOKSTORES

176 BROOKLINE BOOKSMITH

279 Harvard St
Coolidge Corner ⑦
+1 617 566 6660
brookline booksmith.com

Elevating Coolidge Corner's charm is Brookline Booksmith, a haven for book enthusiasts. The bookstore features a range of the latest bestsellers to hidden literary gems, and often hosts esteemed authors. Its warm ambiance, coupled with knowledgeable staff and curated recommendations, create an engaging space for all readers.

177 TRIDENT BOOKSELLERS & CAFE

338 Newbury St
Back Bay ①
+1 617 267 8688
tridentbookscafe.com

Amid the bustle of Newbury Street, Trident combines a bookstore and cafe, perfect for book and coffee lovers. You can easily spend hours browsing their vast selection or enjoying brunch with friends while chatting about your latest reads, all in a welcoming space known for its friendly service and positive energy.

178 PAPERCUTS BOOKSHOP

60 South St
Jamaica Plain ⑦
+1 617 522 3404
papercutsjp.com

Papercuts Bookshop is a small but engaging bookstore in the diverse community of Jamaica Plain. Inside you'll find a convenient maze of bookshelves organized as a circle around the entirety of the store. Each shelf is filled with post-it notes full of book recommendations with summaries and highlights written by the helpful, friendly staff.

179 PORTER SQUARE BOOKS

1815 Massachusetts Avenue
Porter Square ⑩
+1 617 491 2220
portersquarebooks.com

Porter Square Books in Cambridge is a beloved local spot known for its thoughtfully curated selection and engaging author events. The store offers a mix of bestsellers, staff picks, and niche titles across various genres. With a cozy cafe and friendly atmosphere, it's a perfect spot to explore new reads or spend a quiet afternoon.

180 MORE THAN WORDS

242 East Berkeley St
South End ①
+1 617 674 5565
mtwyouth.org

More Than Words is a bookstore and cafe that empowers at-risk youth by involving them in every aspect of the business and providing on-the-job training. With a diverse selection of new and used books, it serves as both a literary hub and a social enterprise, supporting the community.

5 NICHE BOOKSTORES

181 **THE MILLION YEAR PICNIC**
99 Mt Auburn St
Harvard Square ⑨
+1 617 492 6763
themillionyear picnic.com

The Million Year Picnic, the oldest comic book store in New England, offers a dense inventory ranging from mainstream to indie comics in a tiny, old-school space. Founded in the early 1970s and named after a Ray Bradbury story, the shop is great for both comic enthusiasts and casual browsers alike, with a dedicated, helpful staff.

181 THE MILLION YEAR PICNIC

182 **NARRATIVE**

387 Highland Avenue
Davis Square ⑩
+1 617 475 0565
narrativebookshop.com

Owned by an immigrant woman from Bangladesh, Narrative specializes in new and used books highlighting authors of color. The bookstore aims to host events that connect and educate readers, such as author panels and community discussions, enriching the local cultural landscape.

183 **FRUGAL BOOKSTORE**

57 Warren St
Roxbury ⑧
+1 617 541 1722
frugalbookstore.net

Located in the heart of Roxbury, Frugal Bookstore is more than just a bookstore – it is a community hub celebrating literature, culture and diversity. It is the only Black-owned bookstore in Boston, and takes pride in promoting works by Black authors and hosting book signings and social events for the local community.

184 **LOVESTRUCK BOOKS**

44 Brattle St
Harvard Square ⑨
+1 617 286 2346
lovestruckbooks.com

Lovestruck Books, Cambridge's first romance-focused bookstore, offers a curated selection of love stories across various sub-genres. The beautifully designed space features a cozy reading nook, adorned with flowers and even a plush pink sofa, creating the perfect atmosphere for romance enthusiasts.

185 **MFA BOOKSTORE**

465 Huntington Avenue
Fenway ⑦
+1 617 369 3575
mfa.org/visit/shops

Located in the Museum of Fine Arts, this bookstore offers a stand-out collection of books on art, photography, architecture, and design, plus museum gifts like home decor, jewelry, and prints. Open six days a week with free entry, it's ideal for art and art-history buffs, and its collection rotates seasonally.

5 SPECIALTY FOOD *stores*

186 **CURIO SPICE CO.**
2265 Massachusetts Avenue
Davis Square ⑩
+1 617 945 1888
curiospice.com

Curio Spice is stocked with a diverse selection of sustainably sourced, hand-blended spices from around the world. Ideal for culinary enthusiasts and gift seekers, this shop provides spices in various sizes, perfect for personal use or as thoughtful gifts. They also host educational classes on spice blending, catering to anyone eager to explore unique flavors.

187 **POLCARI'S COFFEE**
105 Salem St
North End ③
+1 617 227 0786
polcariscoffee.com

A North End staple since 1932, Polcari's Coffee brings the flavor of old-world Italy to Boston. Alongside its extensive selection of imported goods, freshly roasted coffee, and authentic spices, the shop preserves its original charm with hand-cranked coffee grinders and an authentic atmosphere that transports visitors to an Italian grocery store.

186 CURIO SPICE CO.

187 POLCARI'S COFFEE

188 **FORMAGGIO KITCHEN**
358 Huron Avenue
West Cambridge ⑨
+1 617 354 4750
formaggiokitchen.com/Cambridge

Formaggio Kitchen, an epicurean haven, boasts an impressive selection of artisan cheeses and handcrafted charcuterie, as well as gift boxes ideal for foodies. In addition to its commitment to quality and locally sourced items, the store also educates customers with weekly free wine and cheese tastings, alongside its class offerings.

189 **DRAY**
18 Union Park St
South End ①
draydrinks.com

Dray is at the forefront of the non-alcoholic beverage trend, as the first non-alcoholic bottle shop in Boston, offering a vast array of mixers and innovative alcohol-free beer, wines and spirits. This store caters to health-conscious drinkers and cocktail enthusiasts alike, providing a unique selection for those interested in the expanding non-alcoholic drink landscape.

190 **TAZA CHOCOLATE**
561 Windsor St
Mid-Cambridge ⑨
+1 617 284 2232
tazachocolate.com

Taza Chocolate stands out for its commitment to ethical sourcing and organic, stone-ground chocolate inspired by Oaxacan traditions. The factory embraces sustainable practices and direct trade cacao, offering visitors bold flavors and a chance to watch chocolate-making firsthand. Don't miss sampling the distinct varieties offered at the factory store.

5 stalls to visit at the BOSTON PUBLIC MARKET

100 Hanover St
Downtown ②

191 **LAUREL GREENFIELD ART**
laurelgreenfieldart.com

Laurel Greenfield's vibrant, food-inspired art captures the heart of the Northeast's culinary scene, with iconic regional favorites like oysters and lobsters. Visitors can join the drop-in paint lounge, where Laurel and her team offer guidance as guests create their own masterpieces from a selection of outlined canvases.

191 LAUREL GREENFIELD ART

192 PETERMAN'S BOARDS AND BOWLS

+1 413 377 8962
spencerpeterman.com

Peterman's Boards and Bowls sells handcrafted wooden bowls and cutting boards made from upcycled wood, sourced largely from fallen trees in Western Massachusetts. This sustainable approach utilizes materials that would otherwise be discarded. Each unique piece highlights the natural beauty of the wood, with maple bowls featuring distinctive spalted lines.

192 PETERMAN'S BOARDS AND BOWLS

193 **Q'S NUTS**

+1 617 764 3741
qsnuts.com

Specializing in small-batch roasted nuts, Q's Nuts features inventive flavors like maple bourbon pecans and orange chocolate cardamom. Crafted with natural ingredients and creative seasonings, their snacks entice visitors with irresistible aromas. Generous samples invite guests to explore a variety of flavors, ensuring there's always something new to try.

194 **THE POPOVER LADY**

+1 617 669 5447
thepopoverlady.com

The Popover Lady specializes in light, fluffy popovers, available in savory and sweet flavors like Asiago cheese and cinnamon sugar. Crafted from high-quality, locally sourced ingredients, these versatile treats resemble British Yorkshire pudding and pair with pretty much anything, like roasts, soups, salads, or simply with butter or jam.

195 **HOPE UNLIMITED**

+1 508 205 0555
@hopeunlimitedshop

HOPe (House of Possibilities) Unlimited showcases and sells artisanal products crafted by disabled artists nationwide. The store offers a diverse range of items including jewelry, greeting cards, and photography. Each purchase aids in providing inclusive employment opportunities,and celebrates diverse artistic talent. The selection updates seasonally, providing unique finds all year.

5

FARMERS MARKETS

and local produce stands

196 **BRIGHTON FARMERS MARKET**

AT: BRIGHTON COMMON
30 Chestnut Hill Avenue
Brighton ⑦
abhealthcollaborative.org

Open Wednesday afternoons in the summer, Brighton Farmers Market is an inviting community market with locally grown produce and artisanal goods. This market not only supports local farmers and producers, but also enhances community life with wellness activities such as yoga and monthly family-friendly concerts that include dance and storytelling.

197 **CHARLES RIVER FARMERS MARKET**

1 Bennett St
Harvard Square ⑨
charlesriverfarmersmarket.com

The Charles River Farmers Market at the Charles Hotel operates year-round, convening every Friday and Sunday. During winter, it relocates indoors to red sheds. Local vendors sell a variety of fresh produce, quality meats, and unique offerings like smoked fish, providing a continual source of fresh, local goods throughout the year.

198 SIENA FARMS SOUTH END

106 Waltham St
South End ①
+1 617 422 0030
sienafarms.com/pages/farmstores

Siena Farms, a 75-acre family-run farm in Sudbury, produces high-quality organic vegetables and seasonal flowers like sunflowers and dahlias. The farm offers a year-round variety through its CSA (Community Supported Agriculture) and farm stores, providing city dwellers the chance to support sustainable agriculture while enjoying fresh, local produce.

199 UNION SQUARE MARKET

66-70 Union Square
Union Square ⑩
+1 617 899 5095
unionsquaremain.org/

This bustling Saturday summer market in Union Square features a mix of local vendors selling fresh produce, dairy, and specialty items like candles and ceramics. Start your visit with a morning coffee and pastry or a kombucha, before exploring the rest of the diverse stalls.

200 ROSLINDALE VILLAGE MAIN STREET FARMERS MARKET

Adams Park
(67 Poplar St)
ABCD Parking Lot,
32 Birch St (winter)
Roslindale ⑦
+1 617 327 4065
roslindale.net/farmers-market

The Roslindale Farmers Market, Boston's largest, serves as a vital community food access point, offering free meals for those under eighteen and reduced-fee stalls for local vendors. During summer, Adams Park buzzes with vendors, wellness activities, live performances, and children's activities, transforming each market day into an inclusive family-friendly event.

5 *thoughtful*
GIFT SHOPS

201 BOS. SHOP SOUTH END

623 Tremont St
South End ①
+1 617 997 7097
blackownedbos.com

Bos. Shop is a Black women-owned boutique in the South End that specializes in Boston-themed gifts and souvenirs that showcase the city's creative spirit. With a focus on local artists and makers, it offers a variety of unique items, from apparel to home decor, making it a perfect spot for finding one-of-a-kind Boston mementos.

202 LOFT & VINE

120 Salem St
North End ③
+1 617 816 2499
loftandvine.com

Loft & Vine in the North End offers a curated selection of unique, locally crafted gifts and home decor. Stocked with artisan goods and North End-themed items, this boutique is perfect for picking up distinctive souvenirs and elegant pieces that capture the historic charm and vibrancy of the neighborhood.

203 PLACE & GATHER

26 Common St
Charlestown ④
+1 617 580 8362
placeandgather.com

Place & Gather, a resident-owned shop in the historic gaslight district, perfectly reflects Charlestown's charm and community spirit. Always stocked with cute home goods and Charlestown-themed gifts, it's a delightful stop for gift shopping along the Freedom Trail.

204 **HARVARD BOOK STORE**

1256 Massachusetts Avenue
Harvard Square ⑨
+1 617 661 1515
harvard.com

Harvard Book Store, a Cambridge institution since 1932, is known for its iconic Harvard-branded apparel and accessories, with the quintessential Harvard sweatshirt being a standout favorite. Beyond souvenirs, the store hosts prestigious author events, making it a key stop for both fans of literature and those looking to take home a piece of Harvard.

205 **MBTAGIFTS**

1731 Massachusetts Avenue
Porter Square ⑩
+1 617 497 0737
mbtagifts.com

The official MBTA gift shop, MBTAgifts sells Boston transit-themed merchandise. From T-shirts to mugs and magnets of favorite train stops, this quirky shop specializes in these nostalgic souvenirs. It also features rare finds like decommissioned transit signage, perfect for urban transit enthusiasts and collectors.

201 BOS. SHOP SOUTH END

5
WOMEN-OWNED *boutiques*

206 DECEMBER THIEVES
122 Charles St
Beacon Hill ②
+1 857 239 9149
decemberthieves.com

Led by Lana Barakat, December Thieves in Beacon Hill is a clothing boutique that invites exploration through its eclectic collection of rare, small-batch treasures from global designers. Each piece, carefully curated with an artist's touch, offers a unique and personal shopping experience, blending creativity with individuality in every find.

209 STITCH AND TICKLE

207 FILOMENA DEMARCO JEWELRY

One Bow Market Way
Union Square ⑩
+1 401 301 5382
filomenademarco jewelry.com

Ashley Vick, a skilled metalsmith, founded Filomena Demarco Jewelry in honor of her entrepreneurial great-grandmother. Her studio blends organic inspiration with meticulous craftsmanship. Each piece, crafted from sterling silver, gold, and natural gemstones, showcases Vick's distinct aesthetic.

208 SALMAGUNDI

765 Centre St
Jamaica Plain ⑦
+1 617 522 5047
salmagundiboston.com

Owned by a husband-and-wife duo, SALMAGUNDI offers New England's most extensive selection of hats. The boutique specializes in hand-blocked custom pieces and curated headwear, working closely with independent milliners and traditional hat makers.

209 STITCH AND TICKLE

63 Thayer St
South End ①
+1 617 792 0792
stitchandtickle.com

Owned by Sophie Truong, Stitch and Tickle features Sophie's handmade leather bags, alongside a selection of gifts, clothing, and accessories. Located in the SoWa district, the boutique reflects Sophie's meticulous eye for craftsmanship, blending local artistry with thoughtfully selected items that showcase timeless style and quality.

210 SHAKE THE TREE

67 Salem St
North End ③
+1 617 742 0484
shakethetreeboston.com

Owned by Marian Klausner, Shake the Tree in the North End offers a curated collection of clothing, jewelry, and home goods. Opened in 1994, the shop blends Marian's passion for global design with local craftsmanship and her ever-evolving selection ensures fresh, unique finds.

5 shops for

NEW ENGLAND FASHION

211 **SAULT NEW ENGLAND**
577 Tremont St
South End ①
+1 857 239 9434
saultne.com

Sault New England focuses primarily on men's apparel, accessories, and grooming products. The boutique blends vintage and contemporary trends, drawing inspiration from classic preppy traditions. With a focus on high-quality, American-made goods, Sault reflects the distinctive and enduring character of the region.

212 **VINEYARD VINES**
800 Boylston St, Suite 115
Back Bay ①
+1 617 927 0490
vineyardvines.com

Founded by brothers Shep and Ian Murray in 1998 on Martha's Vineyard, Vineyard Vines epitomizes coastal style with its colorful, preppy clothing and accessories. The brand's offerings, from tailored shorts to patterned dresses, embody a relaxed yet polished aesthetic, reflecting a lifestyle that celebrates both tradition and the carefree spirit of coastal New England.

213 **THE ANDOVER SHOP**

22 Holyoke St
Harvard Square ⑨
+1 617 876 4900
theandovershop.com

Steeped in history, The Andover Shop has offered expertly tailored menswear since 1948, blending classic style with meticulous craftsmanship. With high-quality garments, including ivy-style suits and exclusive tweed jackets, the shop provides made-to-measure services using the finest materials. Its dedication to quality has ensured its lasting appeal across generations.

214 **TRACKSMITH**

285 Newbury St
Back Bay ①
+1 781 235 0027
tracksmith.com/pages/trackhouse

Founded in New England, Tracksmith reflects the area's deep running heritage with its premium apparel and footwear crafted for committed runners. Drawing inspiration from classic athletic styles, the brand merges performance and timeless design. The Boston-based Trackhouse hosts a running club and annual Boston Marathon celebrations, fostering connection among local runners.

215 **SLATE**

54 High St
Charlestown ④
+1 617 398 6323
slatemv.com

Slate presents a refined selection of women's clothing, jewelry, and accessories that blend tradition with modern sensibility. With a focus on craftsmanship and enduring design, the boutique captures New England's understated elegance, offering timeless pieces that are both practical and stylish, rooted in the Northeast's distinctive aesthetic.

5 shops for SNEAKERHEADS

216 **ORCHARD SKATESHOP**
149 North St
North End ③
+1 617 782 7777
orchardshop.com

Orchard Skateshop is a cultural hub for sneakerheads and skaters, offering limited-edition sneakers and premium skate gear. Known for its deep connection to Boston's skateboarding scene, the shop also features a mini ramp and an in-house art gallery. With knowledgeable staff and a unique selection, it's a go-to spot.

217 **CONVERSE FLAGSHIP STORE**
1 Lovejoy Wharf
North End ③
+1 617 248 9530
converse.com

Converse, founded over 150 years ago in Massachusetts, invites lovers of this old-school sneaker brand to its flagship store – a prime destination just beneath its headquarters. The store features exclusive releases, interactive customization stations, and showcases Converse's rich history.

218 **AWOL**
190 Harvard Avenue
Allston ⑨
+1 617 787 0600
shopawol.com

AWOL, known for its high-end and rare sneakers, is a top spot for sneaker enthusiasts. Exclusive drops and hard-to-find kicks, often announced on Instagram, draw dedicated sneakerheads. The store's minimalist design and attentive staff make it a favorite for those seeking the most coveted sneakers.

219 BODEGA

6 Clearway St
Back Bay ①
+1 866 852 6334
bdgastore.com

Behind a concealed entrance disguised as a convenience store, Bodega has been redefining the sneaker and streetwear scene since 2006. Known well beyond Boston, the shop is committed to creativity and fuses art, fashion and counterculture, with exclusive pieces from over 100 brands.

220 CNCPTS

18 Newbury St
Back Bay ①
cncpts.com

CNCPTS' Boston flagship spans three floors, with exclusive sneakers, streetwear, and unique collaborations. With a design that merges retail and art gallery aesthetics, including a hidden coffee shop, the space encourages exploration and community interaction. Its innovative layout and emphasis on storytelling redefines the traditional shopping experience.

219 BODEGA

5 *places for* **VINTAGE** *and* **THRIFTED FINDS**

221 **RETROSPECT**
940 Massachusetts Avenue
Central Square ⑨
retrospectcentral.wixsite.com/links

Retrospect features high-quality, handpicked pieces of vintage clothing, accessories, and home decor. From classic silhouettes to quirky prints, the store provides a nostalgic experience for fashion lovers. With its friendly staff and cozy atmosphere, it's an inviting shop to discover timeless fashion and distinctive pieces.

222 **GOOD TASTE RECORDS**
4 Thacher St
North End ③
+1 617 209 9953
goodtasterecords.com

GOOD TASTE Records is a small yet mighty record shop in the North End, specializing in new and used vinyl – particularly hip-hop, jazz, and funk. Vinyl enthusiasts can test their rare finds at the in-store listening station, ensuring quality before purchase, and the knowledgeable staff is always ready to help customers navigate the inventory.

223 **40 SOUTH ST.**

40 South St
Jamaica Plain ⑦
+1 617 522 5066
fortysouthst.com

Owned by local rock legend Hilken Mancini, co-founder of Punk Rock Aerobics, 40 South St. is a laid-back vintage clothing store in Boston specializing in curated fashions from the 60s to the 80s. With an overwhelming selection of high-quality, affordable retro pieces and well-composed window displays, it's perfect for an afternoon of vintage foraging.

224 **WE THIEVES**

1307 Cambridge St
Inman Square ⑨
+1 857 997 8907
wethieves.com

We Thieves is a woman-owned, conscious fashion boutique founded by fashion industry veteran Sandra Rossi. Specializing in high-end vintage clothing and accessories, it offers expertly chosen pieces geared towards a diverse customer base. It also hosts an annual Clothing Swap & Repair Day, supporting local artisans and promoting a circular economy by mitigating textile waste.

225 **RESIDE**

266 Concord Avenue
West Cambridge ⑨
+1 617 547 2929
resideinc.com

RESIDE specializes in mid-century modern and contemporary vintage furniture, featuring a coveted collection from renowned modernist designers. With its constantly changing inventory and expert restoration services, RESIDE stands out as a top destination for those looking for unique, stylish home furnishings that offer something beyond the typical furniture store.

5 *inspirational* HOME DECOR *studios*

226 **MONROE HOME & STYLE**
207 Main St
Charlestown ④
+1 617 242 2510
monroeboston.com

Set in a revived antique shop in Charlestown, Monroe offers an ever-changing mix of chic, artisanal decor blending traditional, coastal, and bohemian styles for modern living. Owned by design author Donna Garlough, the boutique is curated like a home to help customers envision how pieces enhance their spaces through thoughtful displays and personalized styling advice.

227 **HUDSON INTERIOR DESIGNS**
12 Union Park St
South End ①
+1 617 292 0900
hudsoninterior designs.com

Hudson artfully blends modern and vintage styles, offering furniture from couches and armchairs to decorative items like framed art, pillows, and vases. With unique pieces not found elsewhere – like ceramics by local artists – it's a treasure trove where every accessory feels like art, making it the perfect place to while away an afternoon.

228 ARTEFACT

1317 Washington St
South End ①
+1 857 350 4397
artefacthome.com

Artefact transforms a renovated 1930s Dodge dealership into a light-filled shop of modern yet timeless furniture and decor. Owners Maureen and Sue curate each unique piece – including sustainably crafted Verellen furniture and global accessories – creating a space that feels both sophisticated and welcoming, perfect for discovering distinctive items that elevate any home.

229 PATCH NYC

46 Waltham St
South End ①
+1 617 377 4149
patchnyc.com

Drawing inspiration from vintage craftsmanship and the eclectic charm of New York flea markets, this boutique offers a whimsical array of home goods and gifts. With items ranging in price, the shop features original art, intricately patterned pillows, and distinctive tableware – each piece reflecting a unique blend of detailed artistry and unexpected color palettes.

230 LEKKER HOME

38 Wareham St
South End ①
+1 617 737 7307
lekkerhome.com

Lekker Home, founded by Dutch designer Natalie van Dijk, is a showroom offering stylish European furniture, lighting, and rugs. Named after the Dutch word for 'enticing', the store blends classic designs with innovative pieces, focusing on sustainability and authenticity. The shop provides complimentary design assistance to help customers create spaces that reflect their unique styles.

5 *whimsical*
PLANT SHOPS

231 **JUNEBUG**
211 Main St
Charlestown ④
+1 617 242 2124
junebug charlestown.com

Junebug in Charlestown is a cheerful flower and gift shop, standing out on Main Street with its pale pink exterior and seasonal window displays. Inside, it offers custom floral arrangements, house plants like orchids, decorative pots, and colorful gifts. With its unique selection, Junebug is a local favorite for the perfect bouquet or gift for a special occasion.

232 NELLIE'S WILDFLOWERS

72 Holland St
Davis Square ⑩
+1 617 625 9453
nellieswildflowers.com

Nellie's Wildflowers, a beloved Somerville shop since 1990, sells creative, customized floral arrangements and potted plants. Owner Joyce and her team craft each piece with care, making every bouquet unique. The shop offers a welcoming atmosphere, often featuring Joyce's dog Maisy, and provides friendly, professional service with great attention to detail.

233 UVIDA SHOP

189 North St
North End ③
uvidashop.com

As Boston's first zero-waste plant store, Uvida has a diverse selection of indoor plants, eco-friendly accessories, and sustainable household products, and even provides plant repotting services. Founded by environmental advocate Maria Vasco, the shop promotes conscious living and plastic-free alternatives.

234 ROUVALIS FLOWERS

40 West Cedar St
Beacon Hill ②
+1 617 720 2266
rouvalisflowers.com

Family-owned for over 40 years, this Beacon Hill boutique is known for its creative floral arrangements and beautiful outdoor display of lush blooms and green-and-white striped awning. Sourcing flowers locally and internationally, it offers personalized service and seasonal designs.

235 GREENHOUSE PLANT SHOP

AT: MONUMENTAL MARKET
36 South St
Jamaica Plain ⑦
greenhousejp.com

Greenhouse plant shop offers a playful assortment of houseplants and terrariums, perfect for beginners and seasoned plant enthusiasts alike. While sipping coffee or enjoying a treat from the inviting cafe, customers can browse or get expert care tips from the friendly staff.

OLD STATE HOUSE

50 BUILDINGS TO ADMIRE

5 HISTORIC HOMES
to visit

236 **LONGFELLOW HOUSE**
105 Brattle St
Harvard Square ⑨
+1 617 876 4491
nps.gov/long/index.htm

The Longfellow House, once General George Washington's headquarters during the Siege of Boston and a temporary hospital after the Battle of Lexington and Concord, later became the home of poet Henry W. Longfellow. The building features mid-Georgian architecture, original furnishings, and over 10,000 books.

236 LONGFELLOW HOUSE

237 **LORING-GREENOUGH HOUSE**

12 South St
Jamaica Plain ⑦
+1 617 524 3158
loring-greenough.org

The Loring-Greenough House, Jamaica Plain's last 18th-century mansion, is a stunning example of Georgian colonial architecture. Built in 1760, it has served as a military bakery and hospital, most notably during the Battle of Bunker Hill. Today, it hosts community events like 'Thursdays on the Lawn'.

238 **GIBSON HOUSE MUSEUM**

137 Beacon St
Back Bay ①
+1 617 267 6338
thegibsonhouse.org

The Gibson House is a preserved Victorian row house in Back Bay, encapsulating the affluent lifestyle of the Gibson family through original furnishings and elaborate decor. It serves as a testament to the vision of Charles H. Gibson Jr., a writer, preservationist, and prominent gay figure. Guided tours are available.

239 **NICHOLS HOUSE MUSEUM**

55 Mt Vernon St
Beacon Hill ②
+1 617 227 6993
nicholshouse museum.org

The Nichols House Museum, set in a Federal-style home on Beacon Hill, offers a glimpse into the life of suffragist Rose Standish Nichols. Designed by Charles Bulfinch and constructed in 1804, the museum is furnished with period artifacts that depict 19th-century culture and society. Guided tours are available.

240 **JAMES BLAKE HOUSE**

735 Columbia Road
Dorchester ⑧
+1 617 293 3052
dorchesterhistorical society.org/james-blake-house

The James Blake House, established in 1661, stands as Boston's oldest home, exemplifying Western English post-medieval architecture. This preserved structure now operates as a museum, offering tours that explore the city's colonial heritage.

5 *noteworthy* ARCHITECTURAL LANDMARKS

241 **BOSTON CUSTOM HOUSE**
3 McKinley Square
Downtown ②
+1 617 310 6300 ext 4

The Boston Custom House, constructed in 1847 with a clock tower added in 1915, was Boston's tallest structure until 1964. Originally a hub for maritime duties, this neoclassical building now serves as a Marriott timeshare hotel. Its observatory offers stunning harbor views and is accessible to the public during limited hours for a fee.

242 **BOSTON PUBLIC LIBRARY**
700 Boylston St
Back Bay ①
+1 617 536 5400
bpl.org/locations/central

The Boston Public Library, a pioneering institution established in 1848, merges beaux arts and brutalist architecture. Home to over 23 million items, it boasts one of the largest collections in the U.S., featuring historical treasures from as early as the tenth century. Its grand interiors and vast resources make it a cultural and architectural landmark.

241 **BOSTON CUSTOM HOUSE**

242 **BOSTON PUBLIC LIBRARY**

245 **BERKELEY BUILDING**

243 OLD STATE HOUSE

206 Washington St
Downtown ②
+1 617 720 1713
nps.gov/bost/learn/historyculture/osh.htm

The Old State House in Boston, built in 1713, is the city's oldest surviving public building. A beacon of Georgian-style architecture, it was the heart of the Massachusetts government until 1798. It is best known as the site of the Boston Massacre, but is also where Bostonian's gathered to hear the Declaration of Independence on July 18, 1776. Today, it showcases revolutionary-era artifacts and remains a symbol of America's fight for independence.

244 MCLAUTHLIN BUILDING

120 Fulton St
North End ③

With its cast-iron façade, the McLauthlin Building stands as one of Boston's earliest and rare examples of Italian Renaissance-inspired architecture – a style more typical in New York. Once a manufacturing plant for an elevator company, its preservation underscores its unique architectural and historical importance in a city dominated by brick and stone construction.

245 BERKELEY BUILDING

420 Boylston St
Back Bay ①
lostnewengland.com/2015/11/berkeley-building-boston

The Berkeley Building, an architectural gem from 1905, stands out in Boston's Back Bay with its beaux arts style and ornate terracotta façade. With preserved sea motif decorations, including fish and shell sculptures, this commercial building exemplifies early 20th-century elegance and remains a striking example of the era's architectural craftsmanship.

5 buildings with a HISTORIC TWIST

246 **RESTORATION HARDWARE BUILDING**
234 Berkeley St
Back Bay ①
+1 857 239 7202
rh.com/us/en/Boston

The Restoration Hardware Building in Boston's Back Bay, originally built in 1863 as The New England Museum of Natural History, beautifully combines history with luxury retail. Now a flagship furniture gallery, it retains much of its grandeur, featuring restored original plaster and a glass elevator within the preserved façade of this Civil War-era marvel.

247 **CHINESE MERCHANTS ASSOCIATION BUILDING**
20 Hudson St
Chinatown ②
+1 617 482 3972
sah-archipedia.org/buildings/MA-01-TD1

The Chinese Merchants Association Building, erected in 1951, stands as a testament to the community's resilience and prosperity post-World War II. Despite losing part of its structure to the construction of the expressway in 1954, this landmark, with its iconic rooftop pagoda and 'Welcome to Chinatown' sign, continues to symbolize cultural pride and historical loss.

248 OLD CORNER BOOKSTORE BUILDING

283 Washington St
Downtown ②
nps.gov/places/old-corner-bookstore.htm

The Old Corner Bookstore Building, erected in 1718 on the site of Anne Hutchinson's former home, has a rich history. In the 19th century, it was the base for Ticknor and Fields, publishers of Hawthorne's *The Scarlet Letter*. Now home to a Chipotle, it's downtown Boston's oldest continuously operating commercial building, with revenues aiding historic preservation.

249 EUSTIS STREET FIRE HOUSE

20 Eustis St
Roxbury ⑧
+1 617 442 1859
historicboston.org/portfolio_page/eustis-street-fire-house

Built in 1859, the Eustis Street Fire House stands as Boston's oldest surviving fire house. Originally housing hand-pulled and later horse-drawn fire fighting equipment, this landmark endured over 50 years of neglect. A 2.5 million-dollar rehabilitation by Historic Boston Incorporated has restored its former glory, ensuring its continued presence in the city's historic landscape.

250 GARDINER BUILDING

60 Long Wharf
Waterfront ③
+1 617 227 1576
chart-house.com/private-events-venue/boston-ma

The Gardiner Building, originally built in 1763 and rebuilt in 1812, is the city's oldest surviving structure of its kind on Boston's Long Wharf. Once serving as John Hancock's counting house, this brick colonial-style warehouse has been transformed into the Chart House seafood restaurant, preserving a piece of Boston's maritime history within its walls.

251 LAGOON BRIDGE

5 *iconic*

BRIDGES

251 **LAGOON BRIDGE**
AT: PUBLIC GARDEN
Beacon Hill ②

The Lagoon Bridge in Boston Public Gardens, opened in 1867, was once the world's shortest functioning suspension bridge, now a girder bridge with preserved decorative elements. Its Victorian design and views of the swan boats create a serene, picturesque setting, making it a beloved spot for photographers and leisurely walks.

252 **JOHN W. WEEKS FOOTBRIDGE**
NEAR: HARVARD BUSINESS SCHOOL
From Soldiers Field Rd to Memorial Dr
Harvard Square to Allston ⑨

The John W. Weeks Footbridge, spanning the Charles River between Cambridge and Allston, connects Harvard's campuses and offers tranquil river views. Named after John W. Weeks, a notable U.S. politician from Massachusetts, it serves as a popular spot for viewing the Head of the Charles Regatta, and cleverly conceals utility networks within its structure.

253 DAVID ORTIZ BRIDGE

34-52 Brookline Avenue
Fenway ⑦

The David Ortiz Bridge, adjacent to Fenway Park, was renamed to celebrate 'Big Papi', who was pivotal in ending an 84-year-old World Series drought for the Red Sox. It serves as a key path to Fenway Park for fans and hosts a new Boston tradition where visitors leave locks along its guardrails.

254 LONGFELLOW BRIDGE

From Cambridge St to Main St
Beacon Hill ② to East Cambridge ⑨

Nicknamed the 'Salt and Pepper Bridge' for its distinctive towers, the Longfellow Bridge links Boston and Cambridge with stunning city views. Adorned with Viking ship prows, it honors Leif Eriksson's supposed voyage up the Charles River. Beneath the bridge lies the 'Trophy Room', an unofficial collection of rowing trophies amassed over the years.

255 HARVARD BRIDGE

Massachusetts Avenue Bridge
Back Bay ① to MIT ⑨

The Harvard Bridge, stretching 2,164.8 feet (660 meters) as the longest bridge across the Charles River, is best known for its unique *smoots* markings, a playful result of a 1958 MIT prank. It also gained historical significance from Harry Houdini's daring 1908 underwater escape after being lowered from the bridge while handcuffed and chained.

5 *public* LIBRARIES *and* READING ROOMS

256 **JFK LIBRARY AND MUSEUM**
Columbia Point
Dorchester ⑧
+1 617 514 1600
jfklibrary.org

Designed by I. M. Pei & Partners, the JFK Presidential Library and Museum is situated on a picturesque waterfront in Boston. It serves as a tribute to JFK's presidency, offering a wealth of exhibits, archives, and breathtaking views. Highlights include the multimedia displays that vividly bring Kennedy's era to life and a comprehensive Ernest Hemingway Collection.

257 **MASSACHUSETTS HISTORICAL SOCIETY**
1154 Boylston St
Fenway ⑦
+1 617 536 1608
masshist.org

The Massachusetts Historical Society, established in 1791, is the oldest institution in the U.S. dedicated to collecting American history. For several years after its creation, and before moving to its current location on Boylston Street, members met in the attic of Faneuil Hall. It boasts significant archives, including the first printed copy of the Declaration of Independence.

258 BOSTON COLLEGE BAPST LIBRARY

258 **BOSTON COLLEGE BAPST LIBRARY**

140 Commonwealth Avenue
Newton ⑦
+1 617 552 3200
libguides.bc.edu/bapst

Famed for its breathtaking Gothic architecture, Boston College's Bapst Library is often hailed as one of the nation's most beautiful university libraries. Featuring stained glass windows themed around academics and Jesuit education, and the majestic Gargan Hall, the library offers an inspiring environment for study, akin to Hogwarts' Great Hall.

259 **WIDENER LIBRARY**

AT: HARVARD UNIVERSITY
1 Harvard Yard
Harvard Square ⑨
+1 617 495 2413
library.harvard.edu/libraries/widener

Widener Library at Harvard University is dedicated to Harry Elkins Widener, a Harvard alumni and Titanic victim. Famous for its vast collection of over 3.5 million volumes, including a Gutenberg Bible and Shakespeare's first folio, its stunning architecture and priceless artifacts underscore its status as a pivotal academic and architectural landmark.

260 **BOSTON ATHENAEUM**

10½ Beacon St
Downtown ②
+1 617 227 0270
bostonathenaeum.org

The Boston Athenaeum, among the oldest independent libraries in the U.S., holds a unique collection featuring over half a million books, rare manuscripts, and curios like a book bound in human skin and George Washington's original death mask. Its classic architecture and cozy nooks offer a fascinating backdrop for an afternoon of exploration, though entrance is pricey.

5 HERITAGE CHURCHES *and* PLACES OF WORSHIP

261 OLD NORTH CHURCH
193 Salem St
North End ③
+1 617 523 6676
oldnorth.com

Established in 1723, Old North Church is Boston's oldest surviving church and a National Historic Landmark. Famous for the lantern signal that warned Paul Revere of British troop movements, it is a key site in American Revolutionary history. The church also features an evocative crypt and offers tours showcasing its architecture and storied past.

262 FIRST SPIRITUALIST TEMPLE
26 Exeter St
Back Bay ①

The First Spiritualist Temple, completed in 1885, was America's first dedicated house of worship for the Spiritualist movement, which gained traction during the Civil War for its belief in contacting the dead. This Richardsonian Romanesque structure, featuring ghostly carvings, later transformed into a theater and now houses a Montessori School and restaurant.

261 **OLD NORTH CHURCH**

263 TEMPLE OHABEI SHALOM

1187 Beacon St
Coolidge Corner ⑦
+1 617 277 6610
ohabei.org

Founded in 1842, Temple Ohabei Shalom is Massachusetts' oldest Jewish congregation and a central figure in New England's Jewish community. Its Brookline synagogue, completed in 1928 in Byzantine Revival style and inspired by Hagia Sophia, features a grand domed sanctuary. It's welcoming to diverse Jewish backgrounds and hosts various community events.

264 KING'S CHAPEL

58 Tremont St
Downtown ②
+1 617 227 2155
kings-chapel.org

King's Chapel, founded in 1686, is New England's first Anglican church. Its Georgian stone structure, completed in 1754, replaced an earlier wooden building. The interior features wooden columns and the historic King's Chapel bell, recast by Paul Revere. Beneath the chapel, a unique crypt with 21 tombs contains the remains of notable early congregants.

265 THE VILNA SHUL

18 Phillips St
Beacon Hill ②
+1 617 523 2324
vilnashul.org

Built in 1919 by immigrants from Vilna, Lithuania, The Vilna Shul is Boston's last surviving early 20th-century synagogue. The stone building features rare, folk art murals with Jewish motifs, painted in the 1920s. Today, it serves as a cultural center, preserving Boston's immigrant Jewish past through educational programs and community events.

5 *impressive*
CHURCHES

266 **BASILICA AND SHRINE OF OUR LADY OF PERPETUAL HELP**
1545 Tremont St
Mission Hill ⑦
+1 617 445 2600
bostonsbasilica.com

Rising majestically over Mission Hill, the Basilica is renowned for its Romanesque architecture and the revered icon of Our Lady of Perpetual Help. Built in 1878, it features beautiful stained glass and a historic Hutchings organ. Known for reported miracles and ongoing spiritual significance, it remains a vital center for worship and healing.

267 **CATHEDRAL OF THE HOLY CROSS**
75 Union Park St
South End ①
+1 617 542 5682
bostoncathedral.com

Completed in 1875, this Gothic Revival cathedral is New England's largest Roman Catholic church. The cathedral features striking stained glass, local Roxbury puddingstone, and the largest Hook and Hastings organ. Historically significant, it has hosted services for JFK, and was attended by Pope John Paul II and President Obama, and continues to serve diverse congregations.

268 TREMONT TEMPLE

88 Tremont St
Downtown ②
+1 617 523 7320
tremonttemple.com

Originally the Tremont Theater, this Renaissance Revival structure became a Baptist church in 1896 – the first integrated church in the U.S. It played pivotal roles in the Underground Railroad and women's suffrage movements, and was the location where Bostonians gathered with Frederick Douglass to hear Lincoln's Emancipation Proclamation.

269 ARLINGTON STREET CHURCH

351 Boylston St
Back Bay ①
+1 617 536 7050
ascboston.org

Arlington Street Church holds an impressive collection of sixteen large-scale Tiffany stained glass windows, designed by Frederick Wilson. Completed in 1861 in Greek Revival style, the church made history by hosting the first public same-sex union in the U.S. and continues to be a beacon of beauty and social progress.

270 THE FIRST CHURCH OF CHRIST, SCIENTIST

250 Massachusetts Avenue
Back Bay ①
+1 617 450 2000
christianscience.com/find-us/visit-the-mother-church

The First Church of Christ, Scientist, founded by Mary Baker Eddy in 1879, is the mother church of Christian Science, a religion emphasizing spiritual healing through understanding the divine nature of God. The impressive church complex features grand neoclassical and Renaissance Revival architecture, including a vast domed structure and a large reflecting pool.

5 *innovative*

CONTEMPORARY BUILDINGS

271 **INTERDISCIPLINARY SCIENCE AND ENGINEERING COMPLEX (ISEC)**
AT: NORTHEASTERN UNIVERSITY
805 Columbus Avenue
Roxbury ①
+1 617 373 2000
northeastern.edu/isec

The ISEC building on Northeastern's campus boasts a dynamic glass façade that optimizes natural light and energy efficiency. This LEED Gold-certified structure features a central atrium and advanced shading system. Designed to foster interdisciplinary collaboration, it includes state-of-the-art labs and flexible research spaces, encouraging transparency and interaction among diverse fields of study.

272 **COMMUNITY ROWING BOATHOUSE**
20 Nonantum Rd
Brighton ⑦
+1 617 779 8267
communityrowing.org

This boathouse on the Charles River is designed to reflect the fluidity of rowing. Its two connected structures utilize dynamic building skins that enhance natural ventilation and lighting. The facility includes boat storage and public areas with adaptable cladding that responds to sunlight and user movement, creating a connection with its riverfront setting.

275 DUAN FAMILY CENTER FOR COMPUTING & DATA SCIENCES

273 SIMMONS HALL

AT: MIT

229 Vassar St
Kendall Square ⑨
+1 617 253 5107
simmons-hall.mit.edu/about.html

The Simmons Hall dormitory on the MIT campus features a unique design with large openings that allow natural light to flow through and create a dynamic, breathable structure. Its vertical layout includes communal spaces and voids, enhancing student interaction while ensuring ample sunlight and airflow. This interplay of light and space creates an inviting living environment.

274 INSTITUTE OF CONTEMPORARY ART

25 Harbor Shore Drive
Seaport ⑤
+1 617 478 3100
icaboston.org

The ICA has a cantilevered design that extends dramatically over the waterfront, creating a striking visual impact. The building's dynamic, folded façade employs alternating transparent and opaque panels, reflecting the fluid movement of the harbor below. This innovative design merges the museum's interior and exterior, enhancing its integration with the surrounding environment.

275 DUAN FAMILY CENTER FOR COMPUTING & DATA SCIENCES

AT: BOSTON UNIVERSITY

665 Commonwealth Avenue
Fenway ⑦
+1 617 353 2154
bu.edu/cpo/project/center-for-computing-data-sciences

This LEED Platinum-awarded building features a stack-like design, reminiscent of a tower of books, rising nineteen stories over the Charles River. Its energy-efficient design prioritizes sustainability with geothermal heating and advanced shading. Inside, a vertical campus layout fosters collaboration with open, interconnected spaces, promoting interaction across departments.

5 distinctive buildings on UNIVERSITY CAMPUSES

276 **GASSON HALL**
AT: BOSTON COLLEGE
140 Commonwealth Avenue
Newton ⑦
+1 617 552 8000

A defining structure on the BC campus, Gasson Hall showcases Collegiate Gothic architecture with its soaring spire and intricate design. Completed in 1913, it was instrumental in popularizing this architectural style across American campuses. The building houses classrooms and offices, while its interior rotunda features impressive murals and a beautiful marble statue of St. Michael.

277 **MIT CHAPEL**
48 Massachusetts Avenue
Kendall Square ⑨
+1 617 253 3913
studentlife.mit.edu/cac/event-services-spaces/event-spaces/mit-chapel

The MIT Chapel, designed by Eero Saarinen and completed in 1955, is a cylindrical, windowless structure encircled by a water moat. Inside, a skylight illuminates a shimmering metal sculpture suspended above a marble altar, creating a captivating play of light. This serene space offers a peaceful setting for reflection and worship for MIT's diverse community.

276 **GASSON HALL**

278 AMES BUILDING

1 Court St
Downtown ②

Completed in 1893, the Ames Building is one of Boston's first skyscrapers, and second tallest load-bearing masonry wall structure in the world. Notable for its Romanesque Revival architecture and intricate masonry, the building has been beautifully restored. Today it serves as a residence hall for Suffolk University.

279 MIT STATA CENTER

32 Vassar St
Kendall Square ⑨
csail.mit.edu/about/stata-center

Designed by Frank Gehry, MIT's Stata Center is an eye-catching example of deconstructivist architecture, featuring tilting towers, unconventional angles, and bold forms. Opened in 2004, it houses various MIT research labs, fostering innovation and collaboration. Its dynamic, whimsical design reflects the creativity that thrives within the academic complex.

280 HARVARD MEMORIAL HALL

45 Quincy St
Harvard Square ⑨
+1 617 496 4595
websites.harvard.edu/memhall

Harvard Memorial Hall, a tribute to Civil War alumni, is a striking example of High Victorian Gothic architecture. Its iconic design features a beautiful multi-colored roof and stained glass windows. Over the years, its three sections – Annenberg Hall, Sanders Theatre, and the Memorial Transept – have served as a dining hall, performance hall, and solemn memorial space for Harvard students.

5 SPORT and OUTDOOR entertainment venues

281 **HATCH MEMORIAL SHELL**
47 David G
Mugar Way
Back Bay ①
+1 617 626 1250
hatchshell.com

The Hatch Memorial Shell, located on the Charles River Esplanade, is famous for its open-air concerts and cultural events, including the famous Boston Pops Fourth of July celebration. Built in 1941, this art deco landmark hosts performances from spring through fall, offering a scenic riverside setting for music and entertainment in Boston.

282 **THE LAWN ON D**
420 D St
Seaport ⑤
+1 877 393 3393
signatureboston.com/lawn-on-d

The Lawn on D is an interactive outdoor space in Boston's South Waterfront, offering a fun outdoor setting for events, live music, and community gatherings. Open May through October, it features public seating, lawn games, art installations, and free Wi-Fi, making it a popular spot for relaxation and socializing with friends and family.

FENWAY PARK
FIT FOR ALL TIMES
AURA PAVILION
DELL Technologies Level

283 MATTHEWS ARENA

238-262 St Botolph St
Back Bay ①
+1 617 373 2000
nuhuskies.com/sports/2010/1/28/matthewsarena.aspx

As the oldest indoor ice hockey venue still in use, Matthews Arena first opened in 1910 as the original home of the Boston Bruins. Now hosting Northeastern University's sports teams, the arena has preserved its historic architecture and has witnessed significant events, including Franklin Roosevelt's presidential rally, making it a landmark filled with rich history.

284 OHIRI FIELD

95 North Harvard St
Allston ⑨
gocrimson.com/sports/2020/5/8/ohiri-field

Ohiri Field, named after Harvard soccer star Chris Ohiri '64, serves as a premier venue for university athletics, including soccer, lacrosse, and the historic Yale-Harvard football game. Situated along the picturesque Charles River, its well-maintained facilities and scenic surroundings create an ideal atmosphere for enjoying collegiate sports and competition.

285 RED SOX STADIUM

4 Jersey St
Fenway ⑦
+1 617 226 6660
mlb.com/redsox/ballpark

Fenway Park, home to the Boston Red Sox, is famous for the iconic 'Green Monster' left field wall and intimate atmosphere. As the oldest ballpark in America, it's steeped in history and tradition. Notably, a single red seat in the right field bleachers marks Ted Williams' record-setting home run.

CHARLES RIVER ESPLANADE

55 PLACES TO DISCOVER BOSTON

5 *captivating*
STREETS TO WANDER

286 TREMONT STREET
South End ①

Tremont Street in Boston's LGBTQ+-friendly South End showcases Victorian row houses and premier dining options. This vibrant street is lined with trendy cafes, boutiques, and wine shops, offering a slice of the city's best urban culture. It's a perfect destination for those who enjoy leisurely exploration and delicious food.

287 HANOVER STREET
North End ③

Hanover Street is a bustling thoroughfare that embodies Boston's Italian-American heritage. Known for its non-stop energy, the street is full of traditional Italian bakeries, authentic trattorias, and charming shops. The aroma of freshly baked Italian goods permeates throughout, and you can sometimes glimpse fresh pasta being made through the restaurants' windows.

288 MARLBOROUGH STREET

Back Bay ①

Wandering along Marlborough Street is like stepping into a quintessential Boston postcard. The tree-lined street is filled with iconic brownstones, each with stairs and front yards spilling into the street. The upscale brownstones offer a peek into the lifestyles of the Boston elite, and can often create a longing to call Boston home one day.

289 SEAPORT BOULEVARD

Seaport ⑤

Seaport Boulevard, once a desolate stretch of docks and parking lots, is now the heart of the modern Seaport District. This bustling corridor is lined with contemporary architecture, waterfront parks, and hosts leading companies. It's a hub for innovative art, upscale dining, and nightlife, exemplifying Boston's dynamic growth and modern redevelopment.

290 HARVARD STREET

Allston ⑨ to Brookline ⑦

Harvard Street, stretching through Allston and Brookline, showcases Boston's diversity. From Coolidge Corner's elegance to Allston's grit, this cultural corridor brims with global cuisine, unique shops, and lively venues. It's an eclectic street where diverse cultures and lifestyles converge, offering a rich tapestry of experiences in its bustling retail heart.

291 BEACON HILL

292 CHINATOWN

5 NEIGHBORHOODS *to get lost in*

291 BEACON HILL
②

Beacon Hill is the embodiment of Boston with its narrow, gas-lit streets and historic brick row houses. This picturesque neighborhood, rich in old-world charm, offers Federal-style and Victorian architecture, once home to literary figures like Louisa May Alcott and Henry David Thoreau. You can even explore their former residences along Pinckney Street and the charming Louisburg Square.

292 CHINATOWN
②

Boston's Chinatown is a vibrant hub of Asian cultures, offering an authentic cultural experience with its myriad of Chinese and Vietnamese eateries, bakeries, and late-night spots. This bustling neighborhood is famed for its annual celebrations like Lunar New Years and the August Moon Festival, showcasing its rich traditions and community spirit.

293 CENTRAL SQUARE

⑨

Central Square in Cambridge exudes a bohemian spirit with its diverse mix of ethnic eateries, trendy cafes, and dynamic nightlife. Known for its street art and live music venues like the Middle East, the neighborhood blends academic, artistic, and entrepreneurial energies, retaining an authentic grittiness despite its modern renaissance.

294 JAMAICA PLAIN

⑦

Jamaica Plain, affectionately known as 'JP' by locals, boasts a multicultural scene and artsy vibe. This diverse neighborhood features expansive green spaces like the Arnold Arboretum and Jamaica Pond. Center Street is filled with unique shops and eateries, embodying JP's laid-back, bohemian charm, making it great for both leisure and exploration.

295 HARVARD SQUARE

⑨

Harvard Square, the intellectual epicenter of Cambridge, is always bustling with a mix of students, tourists, and locals. This historic square boasts countless shops, restaurants filled with history, and vibrant entertainment venues. Anchored by the prestigious Harvard University, it serves as a dynamic crossroads where culture and academia converge.

5 urban oasis

GARDEN ESCAPES

296 PEACE GARDEN

AT: ST. LEONARD'S CHURCH
320 Hanover St
North End ③
+1 617 367 0456

Often missed along bustling Hanover Street in the North End, the Peace Garden at St. Leonard's Church is a serene urban sanctuary symbolizing tranquility and spiritual renewal. Filled with beautiful sculptures and floral arrangements, it's connected to one of the oldest Italian-immigrant-built churches in the U.S. and open to all.

297 SOUTHWEST CORRIDOR PARK

AT: HEADQUARTERS BUILDING
38 New Heath St
SW Corridor Path
South End ①
+1 617 727 0057
mass.gov/locations/southwest-corridor-park

Spanning from Back Bay to Jamaica Plain, Southwest Corridor Park repurposes unused highway infrastructure into a commuter-friendly greenway. The park features basketball courts, playgrounds, and community gardens, with extensive walking and biking paths. The Back Bay section showcases beautifully maintained public gardens, offering a refreshing contrast to the surrounding urban landscape.

298 **ARNOLD ARBORETUM**

125 Arborway
Jamaica Plain ⑦
+1 617 384 5454
arboretum.harvard.edu

Managed by Harvard University, Boston's Arnold Arboretum is an urban retreat featuring a remarkable bonsai tree collection – meticulously shaped miniature trees cultivated for over a century. Visitors can admire the delicate art of bonsai while exploring the arboretum's diverse plant species across its expansive grounds.

299 **URBAN PARK (UP) ROOF GARDEN**

325 Main St
Cambridge ⑨
+1 617 491 0709
kendallcenter.com/events-public-programs/roof-garden

Perched atop a building in Kendall Square's technology hub, this hidden rooftop garden offers panoramic views of the Cambridge skyline. Seamlessly blending urban design with natural elements, it features landscaped gardens, modern sculptures, and comfortable seating areas. It's the ideal spot for a tranquil break during a busy day.

300 **JAMES P. KELLEHER ROSE GARDEN**

73 Park Drive
Fenway ⑦
+1 617 522 2700
thefenway.com/locations/kelleher-rose-garden

Located within the Back Bay Fens, the Kelleher Rose Garden features over 200 rose varieties, blooming from late spring through fall. Designed in 1931 by landscape artist Arthur Shurcliff, it offers a romantic retreat and educational space for rose enthusiasts. Volunteers meet weekly to help maintain the garden, and newcomers are always welcome.

5 *free panoramic*
VIEWPOINTS

301 **CONSTITUTION WHARF**
1 Constitution Wharf
Charlestown ④

At Constitution Wharf in Charlestown's Navy Yard, you get the best of both worlds: one side offers views of the historic USS *Constitution*, while the other showcases the Boston skyline with the Zakim Bridge and boats docked in the foreground. It's the ideal spot for a leisurely walk to enjoy the scenery.

302 **LOPRESTI PARK**
33 Sumner St
East Boston ⑥
+1 617 635 4505

LoPresti Park in East Boston offers waterfront views of the North End and Downtown skyline across the inner harbor. Uniquely situated above the Sumner and Callahan Tunnels, it features signs marking their paths beneath the water. Quieter and less crowded than nearby Piers Park, it's a peaceful spot to take in the scenery.

303 DORCHESTER HEIGHTS

South Boston ⑤
nps.gov/bost/learn/historyculture/dohe.htm

Dorchester Heights, a key site in the Revolutionary War, offers commanding views of the city skyline and harbor. Pivotal in forcing the British evacuation, this historic landmark now serves as a peaceful park, with walking paths and informative plaques that invite visitors to reflect on Boston's rich history amidst its sweeping vistas.

304 MUSEUM OF SCIENCE PARKING GARAGE

1 Science Park
East Cambridge ⑨
+1 617 723 2500
mos.org/visit/directions

The top level of the Museum of Science parking garage is an unconventional viewpoint offering an expansive panorama of the Charles River and the Boston skyline. This spot is favored by photographers and those seeking a unique perspective on the city, as well as unobstructed views over the Longfellow Bridge.

305 LOVEJOY WHARF

Lovejoy Wharf
North End ③

Lovejoy Wharf, near TD Garden, offers dramatic sunset views over the Zakim Bridge. This spot features several restaurants with outdoor seating perfect for enjoying the view. A short walk to Paul Revere Park via the Locks Bridge also provides excellent photo opportunities of TD Garden, often illuminated in various colors for special events.

5 WATERSIDE PARKS
for a picnic

306 **CHARLES RIVER ESPLANADE**
Back Bay ①
+1 617 227 0365
esplanade.org

The Charles River Esplanade is a perfect picnic spot, offering plenty of space and scenic options, from grassy nooks along the paths to empty docks above the water. For a quick bite, grab a gourmet charcuterie box from nearby Kured Co. and savor it while enjoying the serene views along the river.

307 **OLMSTED PARK**
217 Jamaicaway
Jamaica Plain ⑦
+1 617 635 4505
boston.gov/parks/olmsted-park

Olmsted Park, part of Boston's Emerald Necklace, is a tranquil picnic spot with shaded paths and meandering waterways. Lush greenery and gentle streams provide a peaceful setting, while open grassy spaces are perfect for park games or gatherings. It's a favorite destination for friends and dogs to relax and enjoy the outdoors.

308 CASTLE ISLAND

2010 William J Day Boulevard
South Boston ⑤
+1 857 702 3884
mass.gov/locations/castle-island-pleasure-bay-m-street-beach-and-carson-beach

Castle Island offers scenic harbor views and one of Boston's most frequented urban beaches, along with the iconic Sullivan's, a beloved spot since the 1950s known for burgers and seafood. After exploring the historic fort, enjoy a casual picnic with Sullivan's fare, or savor your meal on-site while taking in the waterfront surroundings.

309 CHRISTOPHER COLUMBUS PARK

100 Atlantic Avenue
Waterfront ③
+1 617 635 7275
foccp.org

With expansive green lawns and scenic harbor views, Christopher Columbus Park offers an idyllic spot for picnics. The park's majestic trellis, covered in wisteria, provides a tranquil backdrop, perfect for relaxing. As you enjoy your picnic, watch ferries and ships glide in and out of the marina.

310 CONSTITUTION BEACH PARK

799 Bennington St
East Boston ⑥
+1 781 485 2804 ext. 105
mass.gov/locations/constitution-beach-park

Constitution Beach Park in East Boston is a perfect spot for seaside picnics, with sandy shores and the added excitement of watching planes land at nearby Logan Airport. Shaded picnic areas, a playground, and calm waters make it an inviting destination for families and friends to relax, linger, and enjoy a simple picnic.

306 **CHARLES RIVER ESPLANADE**

309 **CHRISTOPHER COLUMBUS PARK**

5 HISTORIC REENACTMENTS *and* WALKING TOURS

311 THE PRINTING OFFICE OF EDES & GILL

21 Unity St
North End ③
+1 617 523 6676
edesandgill.org

At The Printing Office of Edes & Gill, visitors step back into colonial Boston to witness revolutionary-era printing. Live demonstrations on 18th-century presses recreate the production of historical newspapers and pamphlets. Named after publishers of the radical *Boston Gazette*, the shop offers for purchase replicas of seminal documents like the Declaration of Independence.

312 IRONSIDES UNDERWAY

AT: USS CONSTITUTION
267 Constitution Rd
Charlestown ④
+1 617 426 1812
ussconstitutionmuseum.org/underway

Experience the 'Ironsides Underway' aboard the USS *Constitution*, the world's oldest commissioned warship afloat. This unique sail through Boston Harbor immerses guests in early 1800s naval life with a crew in period uniforms and includes a 21-gun salute at Fort Independence. Access is exclusive, offered via a public lottery.

313 **THE DARK SIDE OF BOSTON**

OFFICE:
87 Mt Vernon St
DEPARTS:
corner of Hanover St and Cross Str
North End ③
+1 617 367 2345
bostonbyfoot.org/tours/the-dark-side-of-boston

Delve into Boston's less illustrious past with The Dark Side of Boston walking tour. This 90-minute walking tour, led by passionate volunteers, explores the city's past of crime, disease, and disaster through often untold historical events. It's an informative option to see the city's less celebrated yet intriguing side.

314 **REVOLUTIONARY WOMEN TOUR**

OFFICE + DEPARTS:
139 Tremont St
Beacon Hill ②
+1 617 357 8300
thefreedomtrail.org/tours/revolutionary-women

The Revolutionary Women Tour, typically offered in March, reimagines Boston's Freedom Trail by spotlighting the influential women of the city's early days. It celebrates figures like martyr Mary Dyer and abolitionist Harriet Tubman, weaving their contributions into the fabric of the American Revolution for a unique feminist perspective on Boston's historical narrative.

315 **HARVARD YARD PUBLIC TOUR**

DEPARTS:
1376 Massachusetts Avenue
Harvard Square ⑨
+1 855 455 8747
trademarktours.com/harvard-tour%C2%A0

Led by current students, the Harvard Yard Public Tour is a 75-minute exploration of Harvard Yard and Harvard Square, highlighting the university's rich history, culture, and notable alumni. Combining engaging narratives with insider perspectives, the tour visits iconic landmarks across the renowned campus, offering an intimate glimpse into Harvard's legacy.

317 BRATTLE BOOK SHOP

5 *unofficial stops along the*
FREEDOM TRAIL

316 **SKINNY HOUSE (A.K.A. SPITE HOUSE)**
44 Hull St
North End ③

Boston's narrowest house, the Skinny House, is rumored to be built during a family feud to block a sibling's sunlight and views, utilizing a small inherited land strip. Located in the North End, this four-story testament to spite adds a unique and amusing story to the historical richness of the Freedom Trail.

317 **BRATTLE BOOK SHOP**
9 West St
Downtown ②
+1 617 542 0210
brattlebookshop.com

Brattle Book Shop, one of America's oldest and largest antiquarian bookstores, offers an extensive collection of used books, rare finds, and antiquities. Famous for its outdoor sale lot featuring one-, three-, and five-dollar books, it's a haven for literature enthusiasts to spend hours browsing and bargain hunting, and provides a unique photo opportunity.

318 BEANTOWN PUB

100 Tremont St
Downtown ②
+1 617 426 0111
beantownpub.com

Beantown Pub offers a one-of-a-kind experience of sipping a Sam Adams beer directly across from Samuel Adams' gravesite at the Granary Burying Ground. Adams was a prominent Boston-born radical revolutionary figure and one of the Founding Fathers of the U.S. This local pub blends Boston's rich history with its pub culture, making it a perfect unofficial pit stop along the Freedom Trail.

319 THE BOSTON STONE

Marshall St
Downtown ②

Tucked away on Marshall Street, near historic Boston taverns, the Boston Stone is a mysterious relic. Embedded in a building's foundation, this two-foot granite stone, marked 'Boston Stone 1737', sparks debate over its origin – from a paint mill's grinder to a fabricated landmark meant to draw shoppers. Its true significance remains a puzzle.

320 NORTH END GARAGE

600 Commercial St
North End ③
+1 617 723 1488
pilgrimparking.com/boston-parking-garages/north-end-garage

The North End Garage in Boston's North End is the historic site of the 1950 Great Brink's Robbery, termed the 'crime of the century'. Thieves stole over 2.7-million dollar from the Brink's depot here, executing a meticulously planned heist without violence. This event adds a notorious chapter to the location's seemingly ordinary façade.

5 significant

MONUMENTS *and* MEMORIALS

321 **STATUE OF MARY DYER**
28 Beacon St
Beacon Hill ②

The statue of Mary Dyer at the Massachusetts State House honors her as a key figure in Boston's history. Executed in 1660 for her Quaker beliefs, her martyrdom underscored the era's severe religious intolerance. Her death significantly influenced the region's evolution towards religious freedom, immortalizing her legacy in the heart of Boston.

321 STATUE OF MARY DYER

322 EDGAR ALLAN POE STATUE

Corner of Boylston St and Charles St
Back Bay ①

Located near Boston Common, the Edgar Allan Poe statue, titled *Poe Returning to Boston*, honors the writer born in Boston's Bay Village in 1809. It depicts Poe striding away from the Common, symbolizing his disdain for Bostonians, with a raven by his side, reminding us of his complex but important relationship with Boston.

322 EDGAR ALLAN POE STATUE

323 HARRIET TUBMAN MEMORIAL

Harriet Tubman Square
South End ①

The *Step on Board* Harriet Tubman Memorial in the South End powerfully honors Boston's historical role as a key hub on the Underground Railroad. Tubman, who often visited the city, is celebrated for her courageous efforts in leading countless enslaved individuals to freedom, with Boston serving as a vital passage on their journey.

324 ROBERT GOULD SHAW AND THE 54TH REGIMENT MEMORIAL

26 Beacon St
Beacon Hill ②

Facing the Massachusetts State House, this monument honors the 54th Massachusetts Infantry, one of the first official African American units in the U.S. during the Civil War. Recruited and trained in Boston, the regiment's heroic 1863 assault on Fort Wagner is a significant chapter Civil War history.

325 GRAVE OF CHOW MANDERIEN

AT: CENTRAL BURIAL GROUND
Boylston St
Beacon Hill ②

Chow Manderien's grave in the Central Burial Ground marks an important aspect of Boston's immigrant history. As the grave of the first documented Chinese person in the U.S., it serves as a historical reminder of the early challenges and contributions of Chinese immigrants in Boston and the broader American society.

5 *fascinating*

CEMETERIES

326 **COPP'S HILL BURYING GROUND**
45 Hull St
North End ③
+1 617 635 7361
boston.gov/cemeteries/copps-hill-burying-ground

Copp's Hill Burying Ground, established in 1659, is a historic cemetery that reflects Boston's colonial past and offers sweeping views of the harbor. It holds a notable African American presence, with many free and enslaved individuals buried here. Among them is Prince Hall, an influential figure in Black Freemasonry and the abolition movement.

327 **PHIPPS STREET BURYING GROUND**
Phipps St and Rutherford St
Charlestown ④
+1 617 635 7361
boston.gov/cemeteries/phipps-street-burying-ground

Phipps Street Burying Ground, one of Boston's oldest cemeteries, offers a poignant glimpse into Charlestown's colonial history with graves dating back to the 1600s. This small but significant site features the resting places of notable Revolutionary War figures. To visit, be sure to contact the city 24 hours in advance to have the gates opened.

326 **COPP'S HILL BURYING GROUND**

328 MOUNT AUBURN CEMETERY

580 Mt Auburn St
West Cambridge ⑨
+1 617 547 7105
mountauburn.org

Founded in 1831, Mount Auburn Cemetery is America's first garden cemetery, spanning 175 acres with lush landscapes, ponds, and memorials for notable figures like Mary Baker Eddy, founder of the Church of Christ, Scientist. As a living outdoor museum, it features artful monuments and offers panoramic views of Boston from the Washington Tower.

329 SOUTH END BURYING GROUND

Washington St, between Concord St and Newton St
South End ①
+1 617 635 7361
cityofboston.gov/parks/hbgi/SouthEnd.asp

Opened in 1810, the South End Burying Ground, Boston's first cemetery for the working class and the poor, holds around 10,000 burials, most unmarked. Located on former marshland, it's surrounded by tales of buried criminals and pirates, stemming from its proximity to the gallows, though records indicate it primarily served the city's modest residents.

330 FOREST HILLS CEMETERY

95 Forest Hills Avenue
Jamaica Plain ⑦
+1 617 524 0128
foresthillscemetery.com

Forest Hills Cemetery, renowned for its Victorian design and funerary art, embodies the garden cemetery style. Its peaceful setting includes grassy slopes, shaded paths, a serene lake, and a waterfall. Notable sculptures by American sculptors Daniel Chester French and John Wilson add to its artistic heritage, showcasing its historical significance as an early public art space.

5 ways to explore

BOSTON BY WATER

331 **TIKI BOAT BOSTON**
60 Rowes Wharf
Waterfront ③
+1 617 209 1999
tikiboatboston.com

Tiki Boat Boston offers a tropical escape on the water, combining stunning views of the city's skyline with a festive, Hawaiian-themed atmosphere. Guests can enjoy island-inspired drinks, upbeat music, and a fun social setting as they cruise around Boston Harbor, making it an ideal way to relax and enjoy a summer day.

332 **DUCK BOAT TOURS**
AT: PRUDENTIAL CENTER
53 Huntington Avenue
Back Bay ①
+1 617 267 3825
bostonducktours.com

Led by engaging, quirky ConDUCKtors, Duck Boat Tours offer an informative and entertaining way to explore Boston. The charismatic guides bring the city's history to life with humor and local insights. The tour concludes with a memorable splash into the Charles River, where you might even get to steer the boat.

333 PADDLE BOSTON

333 PADDLE BOSTON

1071 Soldiers Field Rd
Allston ⑨
+1 617 965 5110
paddleboston.com

With multiple locations along the Charles River, Paddle Boston offers kayaking and paddleboarding for peaceful excursions with views of both Boston and Cambridge skylines. Ideal for fitness enthusiasts and nature lovers alike, it's an active and accessible way to enjoy the city's outdoors and experience Boston from a unique waterside perspective.

334 BOSTON LAUNCH COMPANY RESTAURANT SHUTTLE

Reelhouse – 6 New St
East Boston ⑥
bostonlaunch company.com

The Boston Launch Company provides an affordable and scenic ferry ride connecting waterfront dining spots in East Boston, Charlestown, and Seaport. Perfect for restaurant- or bar-hopping, this ride offers beautiful harbor views and a relaxing alternative to navigating city traffic, allowing diners to explore three unique neighborhoods while enjoying the best of Boston's harbor.

335 LIBERTY FLEET OF TALL SHIPS

10 Waterside Avenue
Seaport ⑤
+1 617 742 0333
libertyfleet.com

Offering mimosa brunches and sunset sails, the Liberty Fleet of Tall Ships provides a unique, hands-on sailing adventure around Boston Harbor. Guests can help hoist the sails under the guidance of the skilled crew while enjoying city views and refreshing cocktails – a memorable way to experience Boston's maritime heritage aboard traditional tall ships.

5 surprising TRAIN ROUTES *and* STATIONS

336 WONDERLAND TRAIN STATION ON THE BLUE LINE

Revere, MA ⑪

Wonderland Station, the final stop on the Blue Line, offers direct access to Revere Beach, the first public beach in the United States, and its name honors the historic Wonderland Amusement Park. Featured in the 1998 film *Next Stop Wonderland*, the station connects visitors to an expansive beach with local history and pop culture.

337 OLD TRAM CARS AND TRACKS AT THE BOYLSTON STOP

Corner of Boylston St and Tremont St
Downtown ②

The Boylston stop on the Green Line, part of the first subway system in the U.S., offers a glimpse into Boston's transit history with two vintage streetcars, including a 1951 Pullman Standard. These historic elements, along with the station's original architecture, provide a unique and tangible connection to the city's early public transportation system.

338 **ASHMONT–MATTAPAN HIGH-SPEED LINE**
Ashmont to Mattapan
South of Boston

The Ashmont–Mattapan High-Speed Line offers a nostalgic journey on orange 1940s-era trolleys through Boston and Milton. Despite its 'high-speed' name, the line operates at a leisurely pace, providing a scenic ride along the Neponset River. Its historic charm and vintage streetcars make it a unique part of Boston's modern transit system.

339 **PAUL MATISSE KENDALL / MIT MUSICAL SCULPTURE**
AT KENDALL / MIT STATION
Kendall Square ⑨

Kendall Band, an interactive musical sculpture by Paul Matisse, is situated in Kendall/MIT station. Installed in 1987, it invites commuters to generate resonant sounds by pulling levers on each platform. Restored in 2010 by MIT students, this unique piece adds a creative, auditory dimension to the daily transit experience.

340 **VIEWS OF THE CHARLES RIVER FROM THE RED LINE**
Kendall Square

Between Charles/MGH and Kendall/MIT stations, the Red Line crosses the historic Longfellow Bridge, offering passengers stunning views of the Charles River and Boston skyline. This brief but memorable journey showcases a seasonal panorama, from vibrant fall foliage to shimmering summer waters, transforming an ordinary commute into a picturesque experience.

SOWA ARTISTS GUILD

55 PLACES TO ENJOY CULTURE

5 not-to-miss displays at the MUSEUM OF FINE ARTS

465 Huntington Avenue
Fenway ⑦
+1 617 267 9300
mfa.org

341 **DANCE AT BOUGIVAL**
1883
RENOIR (EUROPE)

Part of Renoir's dance series, *Dance at Bougival*, painted in 1883, beautifully captures the joy and spontaneity of a couple dancing in the French village of Bougival. This masterpiece of the Impressionist movement showcases Renoir's distinctive brushwork, skillfully capturing the play of light and movement, and immersing viewers in the lively atmosphere.

342 **KING MYCERINUS AND QUEEN**
(EGYPT)

The statue of King Mycerinus and Queen is a remarkable example of ancient Egyptian art, capturing the regal and divine representation of pharaonic figures. Discovered in 1910, this nearly life-size sculpture portrays the king and queen standing side by side, embodying the ideals of kingship and femininity, making it a must-see artifact of ancient craftsmanship.

343 **WHERE DO WE COME FROM? WHAT ARE WE? WHERE ARE WE GOING?**
1897
GAUGUIN (EUROPE)

This Gauguin painting, created during his time in Tahiti, delves into profound questions of human existence. This monumental work is a striking example of his Post-Impressionist style, featuring vivid colors and thick brushstrokes that convey a rich tapestry of symbolism and emotional intensity, making it one of Gaguin's most ambitious and celebrated pieces.

344 **PAUL REVERE**
1768
JOHN SINGLETON COPLEY (AMERICAS)

John Singleton Copley's 1768 portrait of Paul Revere is a masterful depiction of the American patriot and silversmith. The painting captures Revere in his artisan role, holding a silver teapot, symbolizing his craftsmanship and connection to the American Revolution. This iconic painting is celebrated for its detailed realism and historical significance.

345 **SLAVE SHIP**
1840
TURNER (EUROPE)

Turner's 1840 painting *Slave Ship* is a haunting depiction of the brutality of the slave trade, inspired by the 1781 Zong Massacre. With vivid colors and a tumultuous sea, Turner captures the horror of slaves being thrown overboard for insurance money, making a powerful statement on human suffering and the fight against slavery.

5 charming MUSEUMS and GALLERIES

346 **ISABELLA STEWART GARDNER MUSEUM**
25 Evans Way
Fenway ⑦
+1 617 566 1401
gardnermuseum.org

Inspired by a 15th-century Venetian palace, Isabella Stewart Gardner (born in 1840) meticulously curated her museum with artworks and artifacts collected from her travels. The dimly lit rooms offer a unique, atmospheric experience, while the stunning courtyard showcases seasonal floral displays. The museum's legacy includes a famous art heist, with empty frames memorializing the stolen masterpieces.

347 **THE COOPER GALLERY**
102 Mt Auburn St
Harvard Square ⑨
+1 617 496 5777
coopergallery.fas. harvard.edu

The Cooper Gallery in Cambridge is dedicated to African and African American art. This small yet impactful gallery serves as a cultural hub for exploring the rich artistic traditions of the African diaspora, with free entry and thoughtfully curated exhibitions celebrating themes like hip-hop culture.

346 ISABELLA STEWART GARDNER MUSEUM

348 **FOGG MUSEUM**

AT: HARVARD ART MUSEUMS

32 Quincy St
Harvard Square ⑨
+1 617 495 9400
harvardartmuseums.org

The Fogg Museum, Harvard's oldest art museum, blends historical and contemporary art with a focus on education and research. Housed in a Renzo Piano-designed building, it features masterpieces from the Italian Renaissance to modern American art, including works by Degas, Monet, and Van Gogh. The museum also houses Harvard conservation labs and research facilities.

349 **MCMULLEN MUSEUM OF ART**

2101 Commonwealth Avenue
Brighton ⑦
+1 617 552 8587
mcmullenmuseum.bc.edu

Situated on Boston College's Chestnut Hill campus, this museum offers a rich experience with its diverse art collection and beautifully maintained grounds. Visitors can enjoy free admission, guided tours, and even take in panoramic views from the rooftop. The museum's exhibitions, curated with scholars from the university, highlight a commitment to fostering knowledge in art.

350 **13FOREST GALLERY**

167-A Massachusetts Avenue
Arlington ⑩
+1 781 641 3333
13forest.com

Showcasing a diverse selection of art from New England artists, ranging from contemporary to classic, 13FOREST Gallery offers high-quality art, jewelry, and crafts to suit any budget. With rotating exhibitions and community-focused events, it is a welcoming space for anyone who appreciates art.

5 *prestigious*
GALLERIES ON NEWBURY STREET

351 **VOSE GALLERIES**
238 Newbury St
Back Bay ①
+1 617 536 6176
vosegalleries.com

Vose Galleries, established in 1841, is the oldest family-owned art gallery in America, specializing in American Impressionist and traditional realist art. Spanning five floors, the gallery offers an intimate viewing experience with a carefully curated selection of works. Its long history and knowledgeable staff make it a cornerstone of Boston's art scene.

351 VOSE GALLERIES

352 **GALERIE D'ORSAY**
33 Newbury St
Back Bay ①
+1 617 266 8001
galerie-dorsay.com

Galerie d'Orsay offers a rich collection of masterworks, spanning six centuries of art history, from Rembrandt to Matisse, alongside contemporary artists. The gallery features rotating exhibitions, personalized services, and a knowledgeable team ready to guide you through the world of fine art.

353 **KRAKOW WITKIN GALLERY**
10 Newbury St
Back Bay ①
+1 617 262 4490
krakowwitkin gallery.com

Krakow Witkin Gallery showcases contemporary art with a focus on minimal and conceptually driven works. The gallery presents meticulously curated exhibits from both established and emerging artists, offering a chic, modern space for exploration. The gallery also engages in research projects like *catalogues raisonnés.*

354 **PUCKER GALLERY**
240 Newbury St, 3rd Fl.
Back Bay ①
+1 617 267 9473
puckergallery.com

Pucker Gallery boasts a range of contemporary art, with a strong emphasis on ceramics, sculpture, and painting from international artists. Known for its museum-quality ceramics, the gallery offers thought-provoking exhibits in a welcoming atmosphere. Frequent new exhibitions and insightful webinars make it a dynamic space to explore.

355 **ROBERT KLEIN GALLERY**
38 Newbury St, Suite 402
Back Bay ①
+1 617 267 7997
robertkleingallery.com

Robert Klein Gallery, established in 1980, is a premier destination for fine art photography. This intimate gallery has showcased iconic photographers like Diane Arbus and Annie Leibovitz, solidifying its reputation as a significant fixture in the world of photographic art.

5 COLLABORATIVE
art spaces

356 **MIDWAY ARTIST STUDIOS**
15 Channel Center St
Seaport ⑤
+1 617 946 4630
midwaystudios boston.com

Midway Artist Studios in the historic Fort Point neighborhood is Boston's largest affordable live-work space for artists. Established in 2005, it offers a unique community for creatives, hosting open studios, exhibitions, and educational events. The gallery presents thought-provoking art across diverse mediums, and is a hub for both local and global artists.

357 **ARTISANS ASYLUM**
96 Holton St
Allston ⑨
+1 617 800 9010
artisansasylum.com

Artisans Asylum in Allston is a creative hub offering makers and artists access to well-equipped workshops and studio spaces for metalworking, woodworking, and electronics. It fosters collaboration among creatives of different trades. Inside, Gallery A2 features member-driven exhibitions, visiting artist showcases, and hands-on educational classes.

358 BOSTON SCULPTORS GALLERY

486 Harrison Avenue
South End ①
+1 617 482 7781
bostonsculptors.com

Boston Sculptors Gallery is an artist-run space dedicated to contemporary sculpture, with new exhibitions every five weeks. Founded in 1992 by sculptors, it has become a premier venue for showcasing diverse sculptural works, from large immersive installations to smaller pieces. The gallery hosts exhibitions and engaging artist receptions, providing a deep dive into the medium.

359 SOWA ARTISTS GUILD

450 Harrison Avenue
South End ①
+1 857 496 5357
sowaartists.com

Located in Boston's vibrant SoWa district, the SoWa Artists Guild is a collective of over 80 professional artists. Visitors are invited to explore a wide range of art forms, engage with artists, and purchase original works directly from their studios. The Guild hosts open studios monthly, helping foster a dynamic and accessible art community.

360 CAMBRIDGE ARTISTS COOPERATIVE

59-A Church St
Harvard Square ⑨
+1 617 868 4434
cambridgeartistscoop.com

The Cambridge Artists Cooperative is an artist-owned gallery featuring handcrafted works by over 180 American artisans. Established in 1988, this gallery in Harvard Square has a diverse selection of ceramics, jewelry, and textiles. Visitors can engage with artists, while exploring a wide range of contemporary and traditional crafts.

5

OUTDOOR ART

installations and murals

361 **MODICA WAY**
Off 565 Massachusetts Avenue
Central Square ⑨

This Cambridge side street, known as 'Graffiti Alley', is a living canvas that showcases a constantly evolving display of street art. Encouraged by the city, artists regularly refresh their work, ensuring each visit offers something new and exciting. It's a dynamic and ever-changing example of urban artistic expression, reflecting the creativity of the local community.

362 **MUSEUM OF MODERN RENAISSANCE**
115 College Avenue
Davis Square ⑩
@museumofmod.renaissance

Originally a Masonic lodge, this Somerville building has been transformed into the Museum of Modern Renaissance, where colorful, fantastical frescoes cover every inch of the interior. This unique space is a living art project, offering an immersive journey into a modern interpretation of Renaissance-style aesthetics, unlike any other.

363 ALL SAINTS WAY

NEXT TO:
4 Battery St
North End ③

All Saints Way in the North End is a hidden alley filled with religious icons and images, meticulously collected and displayed by a local resident. This private, outdoor shrine is a tribute to Catholic saints, offering a unique, spiritual experience amidst the bustling neighborhood, and reflects the deep-rooted faith of the Italian community.

364 ROSE KENNEDY GREENWAY MURALS

Atlantic Avenue
Downtown ②

The Rose Kennedy Greenway's rotating murals and art installations transform air vent buildings and public pathways into large-scale canvases, featuring works by international contemporary artists. These ever-evolving displays infuse Boston's urban landscape with fresh energy and diverse artistic perspectives, highlighting the city's dedication to public art and creative expression.

365 ICA WATERSHED

256 Marginal St
East Boston ⑥
+1 617 478 3100
icaboston.org/ica-watershed

Located in the East Boston Shipyard, the ICA Watershed transforms a former industrial space into a vast hall for immersive, large-scale contemporary art installations. Only open in the summer, the expansive venue allows for dramatic, cutting-edge works, and visitors can enjoy seasonal exhibitions that push creative boundaries while exploring the evolving waterfront neighborhood.

5 THEMATIC MUSEUMS

366 **ETHER DOME**
AT: BULFINCH BUILDING, MASSACHUSETTS GENERAL HOSPITAL
55 Fruit St
West End ②
+1 617 724 8009
massgeneral.org/museum/exhibits/ether-dome

Located at Massachusetts General Hospital, the Ether Dome is a historic operating theater where ether was first demonstrated as an anesthetic in 1846. This site retains its original surgical setup and features a collection of medical artifacts, including a mummy, offering a rare insight into 19th-century medical practices and advancements in anesthesia. Because the Dome is often used by the hospital for meetings, it's important to call ahead of your visit.

367 **ANCIENT AND HONORABLE ARTILLERY COMPANY**
4 Faneuil Hall Square
Downtown ②
+1 617 227 1638
www.ahac.us.com

Located in Faneuil Hall, the museum is rich with military artifacts and memorabilia dating back to colonial America. Founded in 1638, it is the oldest chartered military organization in the Western Hemisphere. The museum showcases weapons, uniforms, and documents that highlight the company's members' role in significant conflicts and its enduring legacy.

368 LARZ ANDERSON AUTO MUSEUM

15 Newton St
Brookline ⑦
+1 617 522 6547
larzanderson.org

Set in a grand carriage house, the Larz Anderson Auto Museum is home to America's oldest car collection. Regularly rotating exhibits trace the evolution of automotive technology and design, featuring classic and vintage automobiles. The museum offers an exploration of automotive history, all within an architectural landmark surrounded by beautifully landscaped grounds.

369 THE WEST END MUSEUM

150 Staniford St, Suite 7
West End ②
+1 617 723 2125
thewestendmuseum.org

The West End Museum delves into the history of one of Boston's most transformed neighborhoods. Through exhibits and programs, it highlights the multicultural community that once flourished here and the impacts of mid-20th-century urban renewal, serving as a vital reminder of the resilience and cultural richness that defined the West End.

370 MUSEUM OF AFRICAN AMERICAN HISTORY

46 Joy St
Beacon Hill ②
+1 617 725 0022
maah.org

This museum offers a deep dive into the life and contributions of Boston's African American community. It features the African Meeting House, the oldest surviving Black church in the U.S., and the Abiel Smith School, the nation's first public school for African American children – both pivotal landmarks in the struggle for civil rights and education.

5 *cinemas for*

INDIE MOVIES

371 **COOLIDGE CORNER THEATRE**
290 Harvard St
Coolidge Corner ⑦
+1 617 734 2500
coolidge.org

A Brookline landmark, Coolidge Corner Theatre offers a diverse selection of independent films, documentaries, and foreign movies in a beautifully restored art deco building. Originally built as a church in 1906 and converted into a movie palace in 1933, it recently underwent renovations and an expansion, preserving its historic charm while continuing to promote cinema.

372 **THE BRATTLE**
40 Brattle St
Harvard Square ⑨
+1 617 876 6837
brattlefilm.org

Located in Harvard Square, the Brattle Theatre has been a beloved single-screen cinema since 1953, known for showcasing retrospectives and themed movie marathons. Specializing in classic, foreign, and independent films, it features a rare rear-projection system. Its intimate atmosphere and thoughtfully curated programming make it a favorite destination for local cinephiles.

373 **SOMERVILLE THEATRE**

373 SOMERVILLE THEATRE

55 Davis Square
Davis Square ⑩
+1 617 625 5700
somervilletheatre.com

Over a century old, the Somerville Theatre is both a cinema and performance venue. Having hosted acts like U2 and Bruce Springsteen, it's also home to 'The Slutcracker', a beloved burlesque version of *The Nutcracker*. With advanced projection capabilities, including 70mm film, it focuses on independent and arthouse films, screening vintage formats and hosting film festivals.

374 CAPITOL THEATRE

204 Massachusetts Avenue
Arlington ⑩
+1 781 648 4340
capitoltheatreusa.com

In Arlington, this historic theater combines modern cinema with vintage charm, offering a diverse selection of mainstream, independent, and foreign films. Established in 1925 with a grand auditorium and pipe organ, Capitol Theatre is now a five-screen venue that celebrates its past by uniquely decorating each auditorium to reflect its original style.

375 LANDMARK KENDALL SQUARE CINEMA

355 Binney St
Kendall Square ⑨
+1 617 621 1202
landmarktheatres.com/our-locations/x019b-landmark-kendall-square-cinema-cambridge

In the heart of Cambridge's tech hub, this cinema specializes in indie and arthouse films, attracting a discerning audience from nearby tech companies and MIT. Since its opening in 1995, the Kendall Square Landmark Theatre has become a beloved venue for independent, foreign, and classic films, hosting premiers and film festivals.

5 theatres and PERFORMANCE VENUES

376 **BOSTON PLAYWRIGHTS' THEATRE**
949 Commonwealth Avenue
Allston ⑨
+1 617 353 5443
bu.edu/bpt

Established in 1981 by a Nobel Laureate, Boston Playwrights' Theatre, based at Boston University (BU), is dedicated to nurturing local playwrights and new works. Home to BU's MFA Playwriting Program, it supports emerging talent through productions, readings, and festivals. The theater has become a key platform for innovative and influential stage writing in Boston.

377 **LYRIC STAGE BOSTON**
140 Clarendon St
Back Bay ①
+1 617 585 5678
lyricstage.com

As Boston's oldest professional theater company, the Lyric Stage has been a key player in the city's arts scene since 1974. Renowned for its intimate, character-driven productions, it presents six plays and musicals each season. Committed to enriching local theater, the Lyric Stage hires and showcases Boston's talented actors, directors, and designers.

378 **BOSTON SYMPHONY HALL**

301 Massachusetts Avenue
Back Bay ①
+1 888 266 1200
bso.org

Opened in 1900, Boston Symphony Hall stands as a testament to exceptional acoustics and timeless design, ranking among the world's premier concert venues. Home to the Boston Symphony Orchestra, its unique acoustics were engineered by Wallace Clement Sabine – the father of architectural acoustics – offering an unparalleled listening experience through meticulously crafted sound-focused architecture.

379 **AMERICAN REPERTORY THEATER**

64 Brattle St
Harvard Square ⑨
+1 617 547 8300
americanrepertorytheater.org

Since 1979, the American Repertory Theater has been a leader in American theater, known for its innovative approach to new plays, musicals, and reinterpreted classics. Nearly half of its productions are premieres, including translations and adaptations, offering a chance to see the next potential Broadway hit. It fosters dialogue, transformation, and celebrates diverse perspectives.

380 **EMERSON CUTLER MAJESTIC THEATRE**

219 Tremont St
Downtown ②
+1 617 824 8400
emersontheatres.org

An opulent theater established in 1903, this historic venue exemplifies the beaux arts architectural style. Renowned for hosting a diverse array of productions, it underwent a remarkable restoration in 1987, returning to its former glory. Today, it serves as a cultural hub for both Emerson College and the Boston community.

5 *alternative* **NIGHTLIFE** *options*

381 **IMPROV ASYLUM**
216 Hanover St
North End ③
+1 617 263 6887
improvasylum.com

In Boston's North End, Improv Asylum delivers top-notch improv and sketch comedy, featuring interactive performances that engage the audience. Since its 1998 debut, this theater has hosted over 10,000 shows, blending audience participation with comedic brilliance. With shows six nights a week, it promises a fresh, uproarious experience every visit.

382 **THE COMEDY STUDIO**
5 John F. Kennedy St
Harvard Square ⑨
+1 857 998 0919
thecomedystudio.com

Perched above a Chinese restaurant in Harvard Square, The Comedy Studio is celebrated for its cozy ambiance and its role in discovering local talent like Gary Gulman. Since 1996, it has been a staple of Boston's comedy scene, showcasing both emerging and seasoned comedians, and offering an accessible venue for comedy lovers.

383 **THE JUNGLE COMMUNITY MUSIC CLUB**

6 Sanborn Court
Union Square ⑩
+1 617 718 0204
thejunglemusicclub.com

The Jungle, a lively community music club in Somerville, was established in 2019 in a converted police car garage. Known for its welcoming atmosphere, it features a variety of live performances, from indie bands to DJs. With its cozy vibe, excellent drinks selection, and friendly staff, it remains a prime spot for discovering local talent.

384 **CAFE 939**

939 Boylston St
Back Bay ①
+1 617 747 2261
berklee.edu/cafe939

Cafe 939 is Berklee College of Music's all-ages venue that showcases student performances and artists in an intimate, no-alcohol setting. It's not only a platform for young talent but also a spot for enjoying a wide range of music genres, from jazz to indie pop, in an inviting atmosphere.

385 **SUPPER CLUB AT CAPO SOUTH BOSTON**

443 West Broadway
South Boston ⑤
+1 617 993 8080
caposouthboston.com/location/supper-club

Located beneath Capo Restaurant, the Supper Club is a subterranean lounge that revives the classic dinner-and-show experience. With a spacious bar, stage, and dance floor, it hosts diverse entertainment nightly, including live music and DJ sets. A highlight is Sinatra Sundays, which features top-notch performers recreating Sinatra's classics.

5 MUSIC *and* ART-CENTRIC FESTIVALS

386 **REVERE BEACH INTERNATIONAL SAND SCULPTING FESTIVAL**
Revere, MA ⑪
North of Boston
internationalsandsculptingfestival.com

Revere Beach's annual sand sculpting festival, occurring over a weekend in July, transforms the historic shoreline into a spectacular display of intricate sand art crafted by global artists. Each year introduces a new theme, attracting large crowds with live music, diverse food vendors, and fireworks. This festive, family-friendly celebration brings creativity to life on America's first public beach.

387 **BOSTON CALLING MUSIC FESTIVAL**
65 North Harvard St
Allston ⑨
bostoncalling.com

Boston Calling, hosted at the Harvard Athletic Complex, is an annual three-day music festival in late May featuring top bands and emerging artists across four stages. With visual art installations and a 100-foot Ferris wheel, it draws thousands of music lovers, both local and tourists, for a dynamic celebration of music and creativity.

388 LOWELL FOLK FESTIVAL

Lowell, MA ⑪
North of Boston
lowellfolkfestival.org

Downtown Lowell transforms each July, towards the end of the month, into a hub of traditional music, dance, and crafts. As the second-largest free folk festival in the U.S., it features multiple stages showcasing diverse music performances, ethnic foods, and local arts. This festival continues celebrating folk heritage from its predecessor, the National Folk Festival.

389 HARVARD SQUARE MAYFAIR

Brattle St
Harvard Square
harvardsquare.com/38th-annual-mayfair-harvard-square

Every spring at the start of May, Harvard Square hosts MayFair, a celebration of the arts, food, and community. The event features three stages of diverse live music, including folk, rock, and funk. Local restaurants set up outdoor dining, and the streets come alive with food vendors, street performers, and chalk art on the streets, creating a festive atmosphere.

390 PORCHFEST

Somerville
beta.somervilleartscouncil.org/porchfest/porchfest-2024

Mid-May, Somerville's porches transform into stages for an annual, decentralized festival that showcases local musicians across various genres. Residents open their porches for intimate performances, and visitors are encouraged to bring chairs or blankets to enjoy the music in a relaxed atmosphere, fostering community connections in a festive setting.

5 *of* BOSTON'S SIGNATURE FESTIVALS *and* EVENTS

391 **FISHERMAN'S FEAST**
North End ③
fishermansfeast.com

This annual festival in mid-August in the North End honors the Madonna del Soccorso (Our Lady of Help) from Sicily. Since 1910, it has celebrated the city's Italian immigrant heritage with religious processions, Italian food, and music. The highlight, the 'Flight of the Angel', features local children performing the angelic descent from historic buildings, culminating in a vibrant street celebration.

392 **HEAD OF THE CHARLES REGATTA**
Harvard Square
+1 617 868 6200
hocr.org

The Head of the Charles Regatta, held annually in late October on the Charles River, is the world's largest rowing event. Spanning three days in October, it showcases elite rowers from around the globe. The three-mile (five-kilometer) course, flanked by enthusiastic spectators, offers thrilling races and an upbeat festival atmosphere, celebrating rowing and autumn in Boston.

393 SHAKESPEARE IN THE PARK

Beacon Hill ②
+1 617 426 0863
commshakes.org

Held each summer in Boston Common, typically between mid-July and August, this free event presents a different Shakespeare play annually. The performances, set in an open-air theater, invite audiences to enjoy classic works in a communal and accessible setting. This tradition continues to be a cherished part of Boston's cultural scene, celebrating Shakespeare's legacy with exemplary outdoor theater.

394 SOUTH BOSTON ST. PATRICK'S DAY PARADE

South Boston
southbostonparade.org

South Boston St. Patrick's Day Parade, held annually on the Sunday closest to March 17th, celebrates both Irish heritage and Evacuation Day. Crowds dressed in green cheer on bands, floats, dancers, and military units along the parade path. Originating in 1737, it honors Ireland's Patron Saint, as well as the city's historic military achievements.

395 BOSTON HARBORFEST

Downtown
+1 617 439 7700
bostonharborfest.com

Serving as one of the U.S.'s largest Fourth of July festivals, Boston Harborfest highlights Boston's maritime and revolutionary history. Celebrated with historical reenactments, a Declaration of Independence reading, and a stunning fireworks display over the harbor, it commemorates America's independence and Boston's central role in shaping it.

USS CONSTITUTION MUSEUM

25 THINGS TO DO WITH CHILDREN

5 HISTORIC ADVENTURES

396 **BOSTON FIRE MUSEUM**
344 Congress St
Seaport ⑤
+1 617 338 9700
bostonfiremuseum.com

The Boston Fire Museum, housed in a historic firehouse, offers an engaging journey through the history of firefighting in the city. The museum showcases a variety of vintage firefighting equipment, antique fire trucks, and artifacts. It's an educational experience for visitors of all ages, giving insight into the bravery and evolution of Boston's firefighting heroes.

397 **USS CONSTITUTION MUSEUM**
Building 22,
Charlestown Navy Yard
Charlestown ④
+1 617 426 1812
ussconstitutionmuseum.org

The USS Constitution Museum offers an interactive, kid-friendly experience with exhibits that bring naval history to life. Children can explore 'Old Ironsides' and get a feel for a sailor's life aboard the ship. Many exhibits are hands-on, making history both accessible and memorable through tactile learning and immersive storytelling.

398 WATERWORKS MUSEUM

2450 Beacon St
Chestnut Hill ⑦
+1 617 277 0065
waterworks museum.org

The Waterworks Museum is an exciting destination for young visitors. It features enormous steam engines and interactive exhibits that teach kids about Boston's water system. Children can learn about engineering and environmental management in an engaging way, making complex concepts accessible and fun for all ages.

399 MAPPARIUM AT THE MARY BAKER EDDY LIBRARY

210 Massachusetts Avenue
Back Bay ①
+1 617 450 7000
marybakereddy library.org

The Mapparium at The Mary Baker Eddy Library offers children an unforgettable experience by allowing them to step inside a visually stunning, three-story stained glass globe. This unique, immersive environment provides a captivating way to explore geography and history, as kids can see the world as it was in 1935.

400 BOSTON TEA PARTY SHIPS & MUSEUM

306 Congress St
Seaport ⑤
+1 866 955 0667
bostonteapartyship.com

The Boston Tea Party Ships & Museum offers an interactive journey back to 1773 with interesting exhibits and live reenactments. Visitors can toss tea into the harbor, explore replica ships, and view the only surviving tea crate from the event. Engaging actors in period costumes recreate the iconic protest, making it ideal for all ages.

5 *interactive* EXHIBITS *and* PERFORMANCES

401 **PUPPET SHOWPLACE THEATER**
32 Station St
Brookline ⑦
+1 617 731 6400
puppetshowplace.org

As New England's first and only year-round puppet theater, this theater captivates both children and adults with high-quality performances and workshops. The intimate Brookline venue ensures every child has a great view. Offering over 300 shows annually, and outdoor shows in the summer, it's a perfect introduction to puppetry for young audiences.

402 **BOSTON CHILDREN'S MUSEUM**
308 Congress St
Seaport ⑤
+1 617 426 6500
bostonchildrens museum.org

Boston Children's Museum is a wonderland for kids, with interactive exhibits that foster learning through play. Spanning three floors of unique activities, including a climbing sculpture and a bubble room, it inspires curiosity in science, culture, and the environment. Special areas for toddlers and accessibility programs ensure a welcoming experience for all children.

403 WHEELOCK FAMILY THEATRE

200 The Riverway
Fenway ⑦
+1 617 353 3001
wheelockfamilytheatre.org

Wheelock Family Theatre showcases family-friendly performances that combine entertainment with education, making it an ideal place for introducing kids to theater. Known for its inclusivity and affordability, the theater welcomes children of all abilities. It's a fun space for families to enjoy the arts together, with classic shows like *Matilda* and *Mary Poppins*.

404 MIT MUSEUM

AT: GAMBRILL CENTER
314 Main St
Kendall Square ⑨
+1 617 253 5927
mitmuseum.mit.edu

The MIT Museum offers children an exciting exploration of science and technology with interactive exhibits that spark curiosity and innovation, perfect for budding inventors and problem solvers. Featuring displays on topics like artificial intelligence and kinetic art, the museum is perfect for engaging young minds in STEM.

405 COIT OBSERVATORY

AT: BOSTON UNIVERSITY
725 Commonwealth Avenue
Brookline ⑦
+1 617 353 2630
bu.edu/astronomy/community/open-night-observatory

The Coit Observatory at Boston University offers families a captivating stargazing experience, allowing them to explore the night sky through powerful telescopes. Open to the public on Wednesdays, this observatory fosters a love for astronomy and science, making it an inspiring place for young minds to learn about the universe.

5 OUTDOOR ESCAPES *and* PLAYGROUNDS

406 **LYNCH FAMILY SKATEPARK**
Education St
East Cambridge ⑨
thecharles.org/our-work/lynch-family-skatepark

Lynch Family Skatepark, located under the Zakim Bridge, provides an exhilarating space for skateboarding, catering to all skill levels. Opened in 2015, this state-of-the-art facility, the largest on the East Coast, was designed by skaters for skaters, providing a safe, community-oriented environment for children and teens to build confidence and hone their skills.

407 **LOUIS A. DEPASQUALE UNIVERSAL DESIGN PLAYGROUND**
AT: DANEHY PARK
66 Field St
West Cambridge ⑨
+1 617 349 4000
cambridgema.gov

This Cambridge playground provides an inclusive, accessible play experience for children of all abilities. With features like wheelchair-accessible swings, sensory pathways, and a splash pad, it caters to a wide range of ages and needs. The playground's thoughtful design, incorporating nature and art, ensures every child can enjoy fun and interactive play.

408 **COREY HILL PLAYGROUND**

AT: COREY HILL PARK

Summit Avenue
Brookline ⑦
+1 617 879 5650
brooklinema.gov/1318/Corey-Hill-Playground

Perched atop Corey Hill in Brookline, this playground offers fun for kids and stunning views of the Boston skyline. With unique wooden structures, water features, and a small park and benches nearby, it's an ideal spot for the entire family to relax, watch the sunset, and enjoy an afternoon together.

409 **BOSTON WINTERFEST**

10 Stack St
Charlestown ④
winterfestboston.com

WinterFest, hosted in December and January in Charlestown, is a perfect winter outing for families, with ice-skating rentals, meet-and-greets with Santa, and a sparkling ice castle illuminated by festive decorations. Emphasizing fun for all ages, it also features an après-ski–style Veuve Clicquot lounge, seasonal drinks and treats, and lively holiday music, ensuring everyone embraces the festive spirit.

410 **SPECTACLE ISLAND**

AT: BOSTON HARBOR ISLANDS NATIONAL & STATE PARK

Southeast of Boston ⑤
+1 617 223 8666
bostonharborislands.org/spectacle-island

Just a 30-minute ferry ride from downtown Boston, Spectacle Island is an ideal day trip and escape from the city's bustle for families and outdoor enthusiasts. The island's 114 acres offer hiking trails, lifeguarded beaches safe for summer swimming, and panoramic views of Boston Harbor from the top of North Drumlin.

5 ANIMAL ENCOUNTERS

411 **A SANCTUARY CAFE**
80 Charles St
Beacon Hill ②
asanctuarycafe.com

A Sanctuary Cafe in Beacon Hill is ideal for kids, offering a safe, playful environment where families can interact with friendly, resident cats. With separate areas for cats and food, it ensures a clean and comfortable space for families.

413 **SWAN BOAT RIDE**

412 **HARVARD MUSEUM OF NATURAL HISTORY**
26 Oxford St
Harvard Square ⑨
+1 617 495 3045
hmnh.harvard.edu

The Harvard Museum of Natural History offers children an exciting journey through the natural world. With engaging exhibits on dinosaurs, marine life, and mammals, children can explore and learn about diverse ecosystems. It is a fantastic destination for all.

413 **SWAN BOAT RIDE**
AT: BOSTON PUBLIC GARDEN
4 Charles St
Beacon Hill ②
+1 617 522 1966
swanboats.com

Since 1877, the Swan Boat Ride has been a beloved Boston tradition, offering families a tranquil cruise through the Public Garden's lagoon. Inspired by the Richard Wagner opera *Lohengrin*, these foot-powered boats with fiberglass swans delight children with views of ducks and swans.

414 **WHALE WATCHING TOUR**
MEET AT:
1 Long Wharf
Waterfront ③
+1 617 748 1450
cityexperiences.com/boston/city-cruises/whale-watch

From mid-May through November, the New England Aquarium and Boston Harbor City Cruises host whale-watching tours departing from Boston Harbor. Families can spot humpback, finback, and minke whales, and might even see dolphins and other marine life. Engaging onboard naturalists enhance the adventure with fascinating facts.

415 **NEW ENGLAND AQUARIUM**
1 Central Wharf
Waterfront ③
+1 617 973 5206
neaq.org/visit/animal-encounters

At the aquarium, children can experience up-close animal encounters, like observing Atlantic harbor seals while learning about their biology and habitat from trainers. Other interactive exhibits include observing penguin species in their daily routines. It's ideal for all those fascinated by ocean life.

5 *engaging*
SHOPS MADE FOR KIDS

416 THE HAPPY JOURNEY TOYS

73 Charles St
Beacon Hill ②
+1 617 936 3917
thehappyjourneytoys.com

The Happy Journey Toys features a playroom where children can explore while parents browse a curated selection of high-quality toys, including wooden options and imports from France. Owner Lindsay has created a welcoming environment that encourages creativity and joy for both kids and adults.

417 BOING! TOY SHOP

667 Centre St
Jamaica Plain ⑦
+1 617 522 7800
boingtoys.com

Boing! Toy Shop captivates children with its diverse range of unique toys, books, and crafts. Kids can explore the various play spots around the store and discover an array of engaging items like fidgets, puzzles, and science kits. It's a standout destination for imaginative play.

418 EUREKA! PUZZLES & GAMES

1355 Beacon St
Brookline ⑦
+1 617 738 7352
eurekapuzzles.com

Eureka! Puzzles & Games immerses kids in a world of challenges with its vast array of puzzles and games. The store features everything from intricate jigsaws and mechanical puzzles to engaging board games, encouraging both solo and group play. It's a dynamic space for young minds to explore.

419 HENRY BEAR'S PARK

17 White St
Porter Square ⑩
+1 617 547 8424
henrybear.com

Founded in 1976, Henry Bear's Park has been a beloved destination for children's toys, celebrated for its emphasis on educational play. The store exudes a warm, inviting atmosphere, often featuring ongoing puzzles. It remains a thriving business by consistently offering high-quality toys that nurture creativity, learning, and exploration.

420 LEGO DISCOVERY CENTER BOSTON

598 Assembly Row
Somerville ⑩
+1 617 702 5593
legodiscovery center.com/boston

LEGO Discovery Center Boston invites kids into an expansive LEGO universe with indoor play areas, exciting rides, and endless LEGO building zones. Kids and adults can explore detailed LEGO replicas of Boston and other landmarks, enjoy a 4D cinema, and dive into interactive activities. This engaging space promises hours of creative fun.

416 THE HAPPY JOURNEY TOYS

LIBERTY HOTEL

20 PLACES TO SLEEP

5 classy

BOUTIQUE HOTELS

421 **ELIOT HOTEL**
370 Commonwealth Avenue
Back Bay ①
+1 617 267 1607
eliothotel.com

The Eliot Hotel, a neoclassical Georgian landmark in Boston's Back Bay, offers luxurious accommodations with a Parisian touch. With elegantly appointed rooms and suites, this boutique hotel is known for its exceptional service, historic charm, and proximity to cultural landmarks.

422 **XV BEACON**
15 Beacon St
Beacon Hill ②
+1 617 670 1500
xvbeacon.com

Set in a historic beaux-arts building, XV Beacon hotel offers spacious rooms with custom furnishings and fireplaces in each room. This exclusive boutique hotel is known for its impeccable service, intimate ambiance, and prime location near Boston Common.

423 **BOSTON YACHT HAVEN INN & MARINA**
87 Commercial Wharf
Waterfront ③
+1 617 367 5050
thebostonyachthaven.com

Boston Yacht Haven Inn & Marina combines nautical charm with refined accommodations. Guests can enjoy rooms with private balconies, soaking tubs, and scenic harbor views. With its inviting atmosphere and attention to detail, it's an ideal destination for those seeking a serene retreat while staying close to the city energy.

424 **BEACON HILL HOTEL**

25 Charles St
Beacon Hill ②
+1 617 865 8020
beaconhillhotel.com

Beacon Hill Hotel offers a charming, intimate stay in Boston's historic Beacon Hill neighborhood. Housed in restored 19th-century townhouses, this boutique hotel features locally sourced art and tastefully designed rooms. With a rooftop overlooking Charles Street and friendly service, it's a cozy hotel that blends modern comforts with historic charm.

425 **SONDER 907 MAIN**

907 Main St
Central Square ⑨
+1 617 300 0956
sonder.com

Sonder 907 Main in Cambridge's Central Square is housed in a beautifully restored 1867 brownstone. The hotel features sleek, modern rooms with plush beds, large windows, and high-end amenities. Its prime location offers easy access to diverse restaurants, cafes, and the energetic arts and culture of the neighborhood.

421 ELIOT HOTEL

5 ARTSY
accommodations

426 **THE VERB HOTEL**
1271 Boylston St
Fenway ⑦
+1 617 566 4500
theverbhotel.com

The Verb Hotel immerses guests in a 1960s rock-and-roll vibe with colorful decor and memorabilia. Situated near Fenway Park, it features rooms with record players and a vast vinyl library. The upbeat atmosphere is enhanced by a heated outdoor pool and musical touches, honoring the site's history where bands like Aerosmith once stayed.

426 THE VERB HOTEL

427 **THE REVOLUTION HOTEL**
40 Berkeley St
South End ①
+1 617 848 9200
therevolutionhotel.com

The Revolution Hotel channels Boston's innovative spirit with vibrant art, including a 65-foot mural by Tristan Eaton. The modern, compact rooms offer stylish accommodations with touches of Boston's history. The lively lobby and communal space encourage interaction.

428 **CITIZENM BOSTON NORTH STATION**
70 Causeway St
West End ②
+1 617 861 4360
citizenm.com/hotels/united-states/boston/boston-north-station-hotel

citizenM Boston North Station marries sleek, modern design with local charm, highlighted by a contemporary façade and local art highlighting Boston's food and sports culture. Adjacent to TD Garden, the hotel boasts panoramic skyline views from its terrace. It caters to busy travelers with compact, tech-savvy rooms and a versatile, spacious common area.

429 **REVERE HOTEL BOSTON COMMON**
200 Stuart St
Downtown ②
+1 617 482 1800
reverehotel.com

Revere Hotel merges Boston's rich history with dynamic art, featuring a Steampunk lantern sculpture, a Boston Massacre mural, and a recycled-material horse inspired by the city's revolutionary past. Its rooftop lounge offers a pool and views of historic Back Bay.

430 **STUDIO ALLSTON HOTEL**
1234 Soldiers Field Rd
Allston ⑨
+1 617 206 1848
hotelstudioallston.com

Studio Allston Hotel offers an immersive art gallery experience. Featuring bold, colorful designs throughout its rooms and public spaces, the hotel showcases works by 22 local and national artists. It also includes unique artist suites, each designed with a specific artist and theme in mind.

5
AFFORDABLE *and* UNIQUE *stays*

431 **ALDERWOOD B&B**
63 Alderwood Road
Newton ⑦
+1 617 965 5950
alderwood bedandbreakfast.com

Alderwood B&B offers a peaceful escape in a quiet Newton tree-lined cul-de-sac. The 1930 colonial home features the host Myra's artwork and travel artifacts, creating a cozy and personal atmosphere. Guests can enjoy a gourmet breakfast, thoughtful conversation, and spacious guest rooms. Myra's Siamese cat, Bubke, adds to the welcoming vibe.

432 **NEWBURY GUEST HOUSE**
261 Newbury St
Back Bay ①
+1 617 670 6000
newbury guesthouse.com

The only boutique hotel on Boston's Newbury Street, this charming stay blends Victorian elegance with modern comforts. Set in three historic brownstones, it features original architectural details, cozy rooms, and attentive service. Its prime location in a sought-after shopping district offers easy access to upscale boutiques, cafes, and a range of outdoor dining options.

433 STAYPINEAPPLE

26 Chandler St
South End ①
+1 857 444 6111
staypineapple.com

Staypineapple Boston is known for its quirky decor, dog-friendly amenities, and fun pineapple-themed accents. Located in a historic South End building, it features cozy, compact rooms with thoughtful touches like fluffy robes and complimentary afternoon treats. Its central location, paired with free bike rentals, makes it easy to explore Boston's charming neighborhoods like a local.

434 HOTEL 1868

1868 Massachusetts Avenue
Porter Square ⑩
+1 617 499 2998
hotel1868.com

Designed to resemble a renovated mill building, this Cambridge boutique hotel pays homage to the area's industrial past with exposed brick, wood, and metal accents. Compact rooms feel spacious with high ceilings, tall windows, and heavy wood furnishings. Located near Porter Square, it offers easy access to Cambridge and Boston's neighborhoods.

435 PROSPECT PLACE B&B

112 Prospect St
Central Square ⑨
+1 617 864 7500
prospectpl.com

This meticulously restored Victorian bed and breakfast in Cambridge transports guests to a bygone era. With period details like marble fireplaces, cut-glass windows, and lace curtains made on 19th-century Scottish looms, it exudes historical charm. Antiques, original art, and a warm, welcoming atmosphere create a unique experience in this eclectic neighborhood.

5 converted

HISTORIC HOTELS

436 **THE LIBERTY HOTEL**
215 Charles St
West End ②
+1 617 224 4000
libertyhotel.com

Once the notorious Charles Street Jail, where famous inmates like Malcolm X were held, The Liberty Hotel, built in 1851, preserves much of its original architecture, including the iconic central atrium. The hotel seamlessly blends Romanesque and Renaissance design with modern accents. The aptly named Alibi bar and Clink restaurant honor the building's history.

437 **THE WHITNEY HOTEL**
170 Charles St
Beacon Hill ②
+1 888 673 3650
whitneyhotelboston.com

The Whitney Hotel, located in Boston's Beacon Hill, occupies the historic 1908 John Jeffries House, once housing nurses for Massachusetts Eye and Ear Infirmary. Carefully restored and expanded, the hotel blends classic red-brick architecture with modern elegance. Its history, combined with thoughtful design, creates a unique connection to the neighborhood's storied past.

438 THE KENDALL HOTEL

350 Main St
Kendall Square ⑨
+1 617 577 1300
kendallhotel.com

Built in 1895 as the Engine 7 Firehouse, The Kendall Hotel preserves its Victorian architecture in Kendall Square. Meticulous restoration efforts, including the rebuilding of two cupolas, focused on maintaining the building's original charm. A curated collection of local art further enriches the character of this carefully preserved historic landmark.

439 HOTEL AKA BACK BAY

154 Berkeley St
Back Bay ①
+1 617 266 7200
stayaka.com/hotel-aka-backbay

Once the Boston Police Headquarters, Hotel AKA Back Bay preserves historic features like original blue lanterns and the 'Police Department' inscription on its façade. Built in the 1920s, the building has been transformed into a sophisticated hotel, with event spaces named after officers, honoring its past while offering easy access to Boston's top neighborhoods.

440 MARINERS HOUSE

11 North Square
North End ③
+1 617 227 3979
marinershouse.org

Built in 1847 by the Boston Port Society, Mariners House in the North End offers affordable accommodations exclusively for professional seafarers. Originally a boarding house for sailors, it retains its historic charm with nautically themed common rooms and restored 19th-century details. With private guest rooms and a seafarer-focused mission, it continues serving mariners today.

PORTLAND, MAINE

40 ACTIVITIES FOR WEEKENDS

5

COASTAL *excursions*

441 **ROCKPORT**
Cape Ann
North of Boston ⑪

Rockport, located on Cape Ann's tip, has charming seaside galleries, lobster rolls with ocean views, and iconic landmarks like Motif #1, often called the most-painted building in the world. Visitors can spend the day exploring Bearskin Neck's shops and stroll sandy beaches before enjoying sunset views from Halibut Point State Park.

442 **IPSWICH**
North of Boston ⑪

Crane Beach's expansive sands and scenic dunes are perfect for walking or horseback riding. From Castle Hill, the grand estate of Richard Teller Crane Jr., there are sweeping views of the beach and Atlantic Ocean. The estate's historic mansion and beautifully landscaped grounds offer a glimpse into New England's past and are worth exploring.

441 **ROCKPORT**

443 CHATHAM

Cape Cod
South of Boston ⑪

Located at Cape Cod's 'elbow', Chatham blends scenic coastal beauty with rich history. Wander Main Street's charming shops and galleries, explore the historic Chatham Lighthouse, and relax on Lighthouse Beach. Often, seals can be spotted on the fishing pier, enhancing the town's perfect embodiment of New England's coastal allure.

444 BLOCK ISLAND

Rhode Island
South of Boston ⑪

Block Island, located off the Rhode Island coast, offers breathtaking views from Mohegan Bluffs, scenic trails like Clay Head, and peaceful beaches like Mansion Beach. Visitors can explore two historic lighthouses, participate in the island's unique glass float hunt, and enjoy local seafood at beachfront restaurants, all within a short ferry ride from the mainland.

445 BOOTHBAY HARBOR

Maine
North of Boston ⑪

This coastal town is the perfect hub for exploring Maine's natural beauty and maritime history. Options include visiting the Coastal Maine Botanical Gardens, embarking on a puffin-watching cruise to Eastern Egg Rock, or exploring Burnt Island's living history lighthouse. Quaint shops, fresh seafood, and picturesque views of Maine's iconic lighthouses complete the experience.

5 HISTORICAL *day journeys*

446 SALEM
North of Boston (11)

Salem is renowned for the 1692 witch trials, where hysteria led to the execution of nineteen accused witches. Key sites include the Witch House, home of Judge Jonathan Corwin, and the Salem Witch Trials Memorial. Walking tours and cemeteries, like Old Burying Point, offer further insight into the tragic events that shaped the town.

446 SALEM

447 LEXINGTON AND CONCORD

West of Boston ⑪

These two towns offer an immersive journey into American Revolutionary history. Walk the grounds of the first battles at Lexington Green and North Bridge, where the 'shot heard around the world' echoed. Explore the preserved homes of notable figures, including the site of Paul Revere's midnight ride stop, and walk the Battle Road Trail.

447 MINUTEMAN STATUE IN LEXINGTON

448 **AMERICAN HERITAGE MUSEUM**

568 Main St
Hudson
West of Boston ⑪
+1 978 562 9182
americanheritagemuseum.org

The American Heritage Museum offers an in-depth look at U.S. military history, from the Revolutionary War to modern conflicts. The extensive collection highlights the impact of technology on warfare and exhibits include rare artifacts, like the M1A1 Abrams tank, and immersive experiences, such as a recreated WWI trench.

449 **BOSTON LIGHT**

Little Brewster Island
East of Boston ⑪
+1 617 223 8666 (Lighthouse Cruise)
bostonharborislands.org/little-brewster-island

Accessible only by a guided boat tour, Boston Light is the second oldest active lighthouse in the U.S. The current structure dates from 1783 and holds an important role in revolutionary history as the center of conflicts between British and American forces. It is staffed by the Coast Guard and provides a unique insight into maritime history.

450 **PLYMOUTH**

South of Boston ⑪

Plymouth brings the Pilgrim's story to life with sites like the *Mayflower II*, a detailed replica of the historic ship, and Plymouth Rock, the symbolic but modest landing site. Step back in time at Plimoth Plantation, a family-friendly destination that recreates a 17th-century village and Wampanoag homesite, vividly illustrating early colonial and indigenous life.

5 ARTISTIC
retreats

451 **PROVINCETOWN**
Cape Cod
South of Boston ⑪

Provincetown's thriving LGBTQ+ community plays a central role in its vibrant arts scene. Known for its inclusivity, the town hosts a dynamic mix of galleries, theaters, and performance spaces. The Provincetown Art Association, drag shows, and local galleries reflect the creativity and diversity of its residents, making it a colorful, artistic destination.

452 **NORMAN ROCKWELL MUSEUM**
9 Glendale Road
Stockbridge
West of Boston ⑪
+1 413 298 4100
nrm.org

Located in Stockbridge, the museum houses an extensive collection of Norman Rockwell's original paintings and iconic Saturday Evening Post covers. Art enthusiasts can tour Rockwell's preserved studio and enjoy rotating exhibits that delve into his process and the social themes of his work, providing a comprehensive look at his contribution to American illustration.

453 **DECORDOVA SCULPTURE PARK AND MUSEUM**

51 Sandy Pond Rd
Lincoln
West of Boston ⑪
+1 781 259 8355
thetrustees.org/place/decordova

Set across 30 acres, this sculpture park and museum features over 60 large-scale outdoor sculptures integrated into the bucolic landscape. Inside, rotating exhibits display contemporary works from local and national artists. The park offers a combination of permanent outdoor sculptures and changing indoor exhibits, creating a dynamic art experience year-round.

454 **MASS MOCA**

1040 Mass MoCA Way
North Adams
West of Boston ⑪
+1 413 662 2111
massmoca.org

Housed in a beautifully restored 19th-century factory complex, Mass MoCA showcases contemporary art on a grand scale. The museum's gallery space features large-scale installations, rotating exhibits, and performances in visual and performing arts. Known for its immersive, thought-provoking works, Mass MoCA highlights experimental art across various media and disciplines.

455 **OGUNQUIT**

Maine
North of Boston ⑪

Home to the Ogunquit Museum of American Art and the historic Ogunquit Playhouse, this seaside town has a flourishing arts scene. Visitors can explore galleries featuring local artists, attend live theater, or walk the Marginal Way, a scenic coastal path that has long inspired painters and creatives drawn to its natural beauty.

5 CULINARY *escapades*

456 **BRATTLEBORO**
Vermont
West of Boston ⑪

Small town Brattleboro's thriving food scene offers plenty to explore. The Farmers' Market on Saturdays provides fresh, local produce and artisanal goods, and don't miss artisanal gems like Tavernier Chocolates, famous for its signature chocolate ganache brick made with Vermont cheese.

457 **MYSTIC**
Connecticut
South of Boston ⑪

Mystic celebrates New England culinary heritage with waterfront spots like S&P Oyster or pizza at the famous Mystic Pizza. Wander through Olde Mistick Village for artisanal treats like Munson's Chocolates, and experience seasonal food festivals, such as Chowder Days.

458 **PORTLAND**
Maine
North of Boston ⑪

Portland's famous food scene, known for New England classics and fresh seafood, is complemented by its vast number of craft breweries. Savor lobster rolls along the harbor, explore the Old Port's specialty food shops, or come to experience Harvest on the Harbor, a fall festival celebrating Maine's best cuisine.

459 **PORTSMOUTH**
New Hampshire
North of Boston ⑪

Portsmouth's downtown offers artisanal bakeries, cozy cafes, and farm-to-table dining, while waterfront restaurants serve New England classics like lobster rolls and clam chowder alongside views of working tugboats in the harbor. Local spots such as Black Trumpet highlight seasonal ingredients, making this coastal town a top destination for foodies.

460 **PROVIDENCE**
Rhode Island
South of Boston ⑪

Providence's food scene thrives on its diverse communities and locally sourced ingredients. Highlights include Los Andes' Bolivian and Peruvian cuisine, Jahunger's traditional Uyghur dishes, and Aleppo Sweets' Syrian-style baklava. This rich fusion of global influences makes Providence a culinary destination for those seeking a wide array of fresh, international flavors.

458 PORTLAND

5 CRAFT *and* COOKING CLASSES

461 **STITCH HOUSE DORCHESTER**
846 Dorchester Avenue
Dorchester ⑧
+1 617 265 8013
stitchhouse dorchester.com

With its bright-pink interior, Stitch House in Dorchester hosts knitting, crochet, and sewing classes for all skill levels. The welcoming environment and knowledgeable instructors attract those eager to learn or improve their fiber arts skills. The owner's lifelong passion for sewing adds a personal touch to this community-focused space.

462 **TUTULAND**
115 Brighton Avenue
Allston ⑨
+1 617 208 8525
tutulandstudio.com

At Tutuland, participants can enjoy creating personalized pieces through the art of tufting, crafting funky rugs or smaller crafts like coasters from yarn and fabric. The hands-on workshops guide you through each step. Alongside tufting, the studio offers other unique craft activities like pouring art and 'decoden', making it a great place for creative exploration.

463 **DAVE'S FRESH PASTA COOKING CLASSES**
81 Holland St
Davis Square ⑩
+1 617 623 0867
davesfreshpasta.com

Dave's Fresh Pasta in Somerville offers hands-on cooking classes focused on making fresh pasta and Italian dishes, paired with wine tastings. Led by Chef Jason, these fun, informative sessions guide participants through pasta-making techniques, including dough preparation and ravioli making. Best part is students leave with both recipes and handmade pasta to enjoy.

464 **RAINBOWS POTTERY STUDIO**
216 Newbury St
Back Bay ①
+1 617 306 6131
rainbowspottery.com

In this creative space, individuals can explore pottery through painting, wheel throwing, and sculpting. The studio offers themed nights like Taylor Swift Tuesdays, where attendees paint while enjoying music from their favorite artist. Whether crafting custom keepsakes or learning new techniques, visitors leave with both handmade pieces and a memorable experience.

465 **MEIMEI DUMPLING CLASSES**
58 Old Colony Avenue
South Boston ⑤
+1 857 250 4959
meimeidumplings.com

At Meimei's dumpling classes, participants learn how to fold and cook traditional Chinese dumplings in a friendly, hands-on environment. The two-hour session covers folding techniques, pan-searing, and tastings of both pork and vegan dumpling varieties. Attendees leave with recipes, lots of delicious handmade dumplings, and the skills to recreate the experience at home.

5 COLORFUL LEAF-PEEPING *destinations*

466 **BERKSHIRES MOHAWK TRAIL**
North Adams
West of Boston ⑪

This scenic drive through the Berkshires features highlights like Hairpin Turn and the Fire Tower, offering breathtaking views of fall foliage. The 63-mile (101-kilometer) route winds through quaint towns and dense forests, over the Hoosac Range, and along the Deerfield River, providing stunning vantage points for photographers and nature lovers alike.

467 **DIXVILLE NOTCH**
New Hampshire
North of Boston ⑪

Dixville Notch's dramatic cliffs and narrow mountain passes come alive in early autumn with bright red, orange, and yellow leaves. The striking contrast between the rocky outcrops and colorful foliage creates a breathtaking backdrop for hiking trails like Table Rock, offering sweeping views. Waterfalls and quiet ponds add to the area's natural beauty in any season.

468 **KANCAMAGUS HIGHWAY**

New Hampshire
North of Boston ⑪

The 34-mile (54-kilometer) Kancamagus Highway winds through New Hampshire's White Mountains, offering a spectacular autumn drive with hardwood forests and scenic vistas. Stops like Sabbaday and Champney Falls showcase waterfalls framed by fiery foliage, while panoramic views from Sugar Hill and Hancock overlooks capture the beauty of the Northeast fall season.

469 **STOWE**

Vermont
North of Boston ⑪

Stowe's Bavarian-inspired architecture, with chalet-style buildings set against a mountain backdrop, perfectly complements the stunning fall colors. The alpine village atmosphere, ideal for hiking and biking, creates a scenic outdoor experience. With cozy lodges and winding roads framed by vivid foliage, Stowe is like an autumn postcard come to life.

470 **SEBAGO LAKE**

Maine
North of Boston ⑪

Sebago Lake's clear waters and vast shoreline are breathtaking in autumn, reflecting the bright forest colors. A fall foliage kayak tour is an ideal way to explore this beauty, taking you through tranquil coves and inlets, and the calm waters provide a unique vantage point to fully appreciate the seasonal landscape.

5 WALKS, RUNS *and* BIKE RIDES

471 **SOMERVILLE COMMUNITY PATH**
Davis Square ⑩
traillink.com/trail-maps/somerville-community-path

Stretching 3.2 miles (5.2 kilometers) from Davis Square to East Cambridge, the Somerville Community Path is perfect for an urban adventure. Lined with community gardens and local art, the paved trail offers a scenic, urban route that connects with other multi-use paths. Its smooth surface and greenery make it a popular spot for exercise and commuting.

472 **JAMAICA POND**
Jamaica Plain ⑦
emeraldnecklace.org/park-overview/jamaica-pond

The 1.5-mile (2.4-kilometer) path around Jamaica Pond in Jamaica Plain is a serene setting for a leisurely walk or job. Part of the Emerald Necklace designed by Frederick Law Olmsted, the trail is surrounded by greenery, making it a peaceful spot to enjoy scenic water views, a coffee, or a conversation with a friend.

473 **BLUE HILLS RESERVATION**

725 Hillside St
Milton
South of Boston ⑪
+1 617 698 1802
mass.gov/locations/blue-hills-reservation

Just outside Boston, Blue Hills Reservation offers over 125 miles (200 kilometers) of trails for hiking, biking, and winter sports. Its varied terrain, from hills to marshes, suits all skill levels. The reservation features scenic views, including city skylines from Great Blue Hill, making it a popular year-round destination for outdoor enthusiasts close to the city.

474 **WORLD'S END**

Martin's Lane
Hingham
South of Boston ⑪
+1 781 740 6665
thetrustees.org/place/worlds-end-hingham

World's End, a 251-acre peninsula in Hingham, invites visitors to explore its scenic carriage paths and coastal drumlins, designed by Frederick Law Olmsted. The landscape blends open meadows, rocky shorelines, and views of the Boston skyline, making it ideal for strolling, horseback riding, or simply unwinding.

475 **FRESH POND RESERVATION**

250 Fresh Pond Parkway
West Cambridge ⑨
+1 617 349 4770
cambridgema.gov/water/freshpond reservation

Encircling a glacial pond, this 2.5-mile (4-kilometer) trail offers a serene setting for walking, running, or cycling in Cambridge. This natural reservoir, surrounded by over a hundred acres of protected open space, is both a crucial water supply and a refuge for wildlife, great for birdwatchers, naturalists, and those seeking a peaceful urban escape.

5 WELLNESS *and* GLAMPING *retreats*

476 **KRIPALU CENTER FOR YOGA & HEALTH**
57 Interlaken Rd
Stockbridge, MA
West of Boston ⑪
+1 413 448 3500
kripalu.org

Located in the Berkshires, Kripalu aims to deliver a transformative escape with classes focused on yoga, mindfulness, and personal growth. Spanning over 100 acres, it provides a variety of immersive programs, from movement classes to outdoor activities like hiking and kayaking. Guests enjoy nutritious meals, serene accommodations, and expert-led sessions by visiting teachers.

477 **SANDY PINES CAMPGROUND**
277 Mills Rd
Kennebunkport, Maine
North of Boston ⑪
+1 207 967 2483
sandypinescamping.com

Sandy Pines in Kennebunkport offers a range of camping experiences, from traditional tent sites to luxurious glamping accommodations with real beds, air conditioning, and stylish decor. Nestled near a scenic salt marsh, the campground provides access to kayaking, hiking, and a saltwater pool, creating a perfect blend of nature and comfort for all campers.

478 **HUTTOPIA WHITE MOUNTAINS**

Pine Knoll Rd
Albany, New Hampshire
North of Boston ⑪
+1 603 447 3131
canada-usa.huttopia.com/site/white-mountains

Tucked in a lakeside forest, this French-inspired glamping retreat offers wood-and-canvas tents, a heated pool, and activities for all ages, from swimming to tubing on the nearby river. Guests can enjoy homemade flatbread pizzas from a converted Airstream or relax with crepes and drinks by the peaceful lakeside.

479 **WINVIAN FARM**

155 Alain White Rd
Morris, Connecticut
South of Boston ⑪
+1 860 567 9600
winvian.com

Amidst the Litchfield Hills, Winvian Farm is an unconventional getaway with eighteen uniquely themed cottages, from a treehouse to a repurposed helicopter. Each cottage blends creativity with luxury, while the on-site farm-to-table dining and spa provide indulgent relaxation. Surrounded by nature, guests can explore the outdoors or the seclusion of this distinctive retreat.

480 **HIDDEN POND**

354 Goose Rocks Rd
Kennebunkport, Maine
North of Boston ⑪
+1 888 967 90 50
hiddenpondmaine.com

Hidden Pond provides a peaceful escape with luxurious cottages, treetop lodges, and bungalows designed for comfort. Guests can enjoy outdoor showers and private porches, or a range of holistic activities like garden-to-table cooking, morning yoga, and bike rides to the beach, making it a fun coastal retreat.

BOSTON COMMON

20 RANDOM FACTS AND URBAN DETAILS

5 FILMS and BOOKS set in Boston

481 THE TOWN

Charlestown ④

The Town is a quintessential Boston film set in Charlestown, once notorious for having the most bank robbers per capita. Released in 2010 and directed by Ben Affleck, it stars Affleck alongside actors Jeremy Renner, Jon Hamm, and Blake Lively. Filmed on location, it showcases Charlestown's gritty history and unique character.

482 GOOD WILL HUNTING

Cambridge and Boston

Released in 1997, *Good Will Hunting* is set around the MIT and Harvard campuses in Cambridge, following a brilliant yet troubled janitor from South Boston. Co-written by and starring Matt Damon and Ben Affleck, it also highlights iconic Boston landmarks like the Public Garden and the L Street Tavern.

483 THE SOCIAL NETWORK

Harvard University
Harvard Square ⑨

Filmed partly in Cambridge, *The Social Network* tells the story of Facebook's creation by Mark Zuckerberg during his time as a Harvard student. Released in 2010, the film stars Jesse Eisenberg, Andrew Garfield, and Justin Timberlake, with key scenes shot around Harvard's campus, connecting the film to Boston's academic spirit.

484 THE HANDMAID'S TALE

Cambridge ⑨

Written in 1985 by Margaret Atwood, *The Handmaid's Tale* is set in Gilead, a totalitarian regime replacing the United States. The novel references landmarks and streets in Cambridge, including Harvard University and areas near the Charles River.

485 FEVER PITCH

Fenway Park ⑦

Fever Pitch, directed by the Farrelly Brothers, was released in 2005 and stars Drew Barrymore and Jimmy Fallon. Filmed at Fenway Park and throughout Boston, it depicts a die-hard Red Sox fan during the team's 2004 World Series season, which ended an 86-year championship drought and became a historic moment for the city.

5 *intriguing*

HISTORIC EVENTS

486 **CHRISTMAS BAN**
1659–1684

In 1659, Boston's Puritans banned Christmas, viewing festive celebrations as un-Christian and imposing fines of five shillings on anyone caught observing the holiday. This strict prohibition reflected the Puritans' austere religious beliefs. However, as attitudes shifted, the ban was repealed in 1681, marking a turning point in the community's approach to public celebrations and religious expression.

487 **GREAT MOLASSES FLOOD**
1919
North End ③

In 1919, a ruptured tank unleashed a massive wave of molasses through Boston's North End, causing widespread destruction. Known as the Great Molasses Flood, the sticky disaster claimed 21 lives, injured over 100 people and left the area reportedly smelling of molasses for years, becoming one of the city's most unusual and tragic events.

488 **THE SPUNKER SOCIETY AT HARVARD**
CIRCA 1770
Harvard University
Harvard Square ⑨

Around 1770, Harvard medical students formed the Spunker Society, a secret group dedicated to procuring corpses for study due to a shortage of legal cadavers. This clandestine effort underscored the challenges of advancing medical education in an era with strict laws and limited resources for anatomical research.

489 **CITY OF SALISBURY SHIPWRECK**
1938
Graves Light Station
Offshore

The City of Salisbury freighter, carrying exotic animals from India, ran aground near Graves Light in Boston Harbor during thick fog. Remarkably, all animals and crew were safely rescued. Today, the submerged wreck near Graves Light is a popular spot for divers, offering a unique glimpse into this unusual maritime incident.

490 **BOSTON MASSACRE**
1770
AT: THE OLD STATE HOUSE
206 Washington St
Downtown ②
+1 617 720 1713
nps.gov/bost/learn/historyculture/osh.htm

On March 5, 1770, British troops fired into a crowd near the Old State House, killing five colonists. Provoked by a mob hurling insults and projectiles, the soldiers responded in the chaos. Dubbed the *Boston Massacre*, Patriot leaders like Samuel Adams leveraged it to incite anti-British sentiment, while Britain referred to it as the *Incident on King Street* to diminish its significance.

5 CITYSCAPE *and* ARCHITECTURAL QUIRKS

491 **BIG DIG**

Before the Big Dig, the elevated Central Artery highway ran through downtown Boston, connecting the Zakim Bridge to the Southeast Expressway. This massive project, completed in 2007, moved the highway underground, creating parks and green spaces in its place. It stands as one of the most complex and costly U.S. highway projects, drastically improving urban aesthetics and functionality.

492 **THE SACRED COD**
AT: MASSACHUSETTS STATE HOUSE
24 Beacon St
Beacon Hill ②

Inside the Massachusetts State House, the House of Representatives chamber is adorned with 'The Sacred Cod'. This four-foot-eleven-inch (150-centimeter) carved wood codfish symbolizes the vital role of the cod-fishing industry in the state's economy during the late 1700s.

493 **REPLICA OF THE VENETIAN DOGE'S PALACE**

AT: NORTH END BRANCH OF THE BOSTON PUBLIC LIBRARY

25 Parmenter St
North End ③

Inside the North End branch of the Boston Public Library, there is a meticulous replica of the Venetian Doge's Palace. This project, initially destroyed and then recreated, reflects the passion of Miss Henrietta Macy, a Bostonian who dedicated her life to replicating this Venetian masterpiece.

494 **ST. STEPHEN'S CHURCH**

401 Hanover St
North End ③

St. Stephen's Church, built in 1804, stands as the last remaining Boston church designed by Charles Bulfinch, America's first professional architect. Its Federal architectural style features signature symmetry and classical details emblematic of the era. Bulfinch, whose works include the Massachusetts State House and the US Capitol, greatly influenced early American architecture.

495 **JOHN HANCOCK TOWER**

120 St James Avenue
Back Bay ①

When the John Hancock Tower, Boston's tallest building at 790 feet (240m) and 60 stories, was completed in the 1970s, high winds caused its windows to fall out, leading to the replacement of all 10,344 panes. This architectural mishap, along with other setbacks that plagued the building's construction, have become a part of local lore.

5 BOSTON FIRSTS

496 **FIRST SUBWAY SYSTEM**
1897

Boston inaugurated the first subway system in the United States in 1897, revolutionizing public transportation. The Tremont Street Subway was the first tunnel in North America and the third-oldest still in use worldwide today. It alleviated street traffic and set a precedent for other cities.

497 **BOSTON COMMON**
1634
139 Tremont St
Beacon Hill ②

Boston Common, established in 1634, is America's first public park and a National Historic Landmark. Once a grazing pasture, it evolved into a site for public events, military drills, and protests, including a civil rights rally led by Martin Luther King Jr. Today, it offers open spaces for recreation and relaxation, with landmarks like the Frog Pond and the Parkman Bandstand.

498 THE TREMONT HOUSE

1829

Thought to be one of America's first modern hotels, The Tremont House pioneered features like indoor plumbing, locked guest rooms, and bellboy service, setting new standards in the hospitality industry. The building, which was located at 73 Tremont Street, was demolished in 1895 and replaced by an office building.

499 CHARLES WILLIAMS JR. HOUSE

1877

1 Arlington St
Somerville ⑩

In 1877, Charles Williams Jr.'s house became the first in the world with a permanent telephone and was issued numbers 1 and 2 by the Bell Telephone Company. Connected to Williams' shop at 109 Court Street, the setup enabled Alexander Graham Bell to test early telephone prototypes, marking the site as a key location in the history of communication.

500 SCHRAFFT CANDY FACTORY

1861

529 Main St
Charlestown ④

The Schrafft Candy Company in Charlestown was a leading candy producer in the late 19th century, famous for chocolates, cakes and inventing the jelly bean, which were marketed as ideal gifts for Union soldiers during the Civil War. The historic factory façade and neon Schrafft's sign still remain in Charlestown, but the building was repurposed into offices.

LAGOON BRIDGE

INDEX

COLOPHON

EDITING *and* COMPOSING – Natalia Ivanytsky
GRAPHIC DESIGN – Joke Gossé and doublebill.design
PHOTOGRAPHY – Claudia Uripos
COVER IMAGE – Beacon Hill (secret 291)

The addresses in this book have been selected after thorough independent research by the author, in collaboration with Luster Publishing. The selection is solely based on personal evaluation of the business by the author. Nothing in this book was published in exchange for payment or benefits of any kind.

D/2025/12.005/4
ISBN 9789460583827
NUR 513, 510

lusterpublishing.com – THE500HIDDENSECRETS.COM
info@lusterpublishing.com

Printed in Italy by Printer Trento.

FSC www.fsc.org MIX Paper | Supporting responsible forestry FSC® C015829